Celebrate Nature!

Also by Angela Schmidt Fishbaugh

Seeking Balance in an Unbalanced World: A Teacher's Journey

Celebrate Nature!

Activities for Every Season

Angela Schmidt Fishbaugh

 **Redleaf Press®**
www.redleafpress.org
800-423-8309

Published by Redleaf Press
10 Yorkton Court
St. Paul, MN 55117
www.redleafpress.org

© 2011 by Angela Schmidt Fishbaugh

First edition 2011
Cover design by Jim Handrigan
Cover photographs except for winter and fall by Jim Handrigan
Author photograph on back cover by Upstate Portraits, LLC
Interior typeset in ITC New Baskerville and designed by Michelle Cook/
4 Seasons Book Design
Photos on pages 17, 18, 23, and 37 by Lois Deming
Printed in the United States of America
18   17   16   15   14   13   12   11   1   2   3   4   5   6   7   8

Library of Congress Cataloging-in-Publication Data
Fishbaugh, Angela Schmidt.
Celebrate nature! : activities for every season / Angela Schmidt Fishbaugh. —
1st ed.
      p. cm.
Includes bibliographical references.
ISBN 978-1-60554-034-4 (alk. paper)
1. Science—Study and teaching (Early childhood)—Activity programs.
2. Early childhood education—Activity programs. 3. Nature study. 4. Early
childhood development. I. Title.
LB1139.5.S35F47 2011
372.35'7—dc22   2010042834

Printed on acid-free paper

To those children who desperately need the chance to love nature,
and to those who provide them with the chance to do so

Contents

Acknowledgments

Thank you to my children, who unknowingly help me strive to be my best self. To my husband, for cooking most Thursday evenings so I can fulfill my purpose by writing. To all my family members and lifelong friends, who shout approval to me from whatever end of the country you are in. To my best friends at work, who make me laugh on my worst days and help me through school and all of life's circumstances. You make today's teaching profession a wonderful journey. I treasure all of you supporting my mission of wellness for today's children.

And to my top supporters, all the children who wave and holler, "Mrs. Fishbaugh, Mrs. Fishbaugh!" You shout it from your buses, on the playground, in the hallways, and from your parents' cars as you leave the school. I adore your natural spontaneity, your aliveness, and your gusto! Thank you, everyone, for all your love!

It is important for me also to acknowledge my favorite mothers. First, I offer this endeavor to Mother Earth. You alone have taught me about miracles. From my birth through adulthood, you have been my favorite teacher in this life. I know you are proud of this creation, and I offer this book in your honor to the children of this world.

To my mother, who, when at her wit's end and with no patience left to give, would send me outside to nature's wisdom. Thank you for caring enough to demand that I go outside! I became a natural fixture of the outdoors because of your hardy love!

To all the past and present mother figures in my life—Karen; Aunt Eva; my godmother, Victoria; my sister-in-law Melissa; and the mothers of Hollister Street, especially Joyce, who loved me unconditionally—I am grateful to you. Your motherly gestures and unique natures have helped shape my own motherhood experience. I treasure each of your distinct dispositions more than you will ever know.

Finally, to all mothers—and nurturing fathers: I believe in you. I know the profound responsibilities of parenting. My hope is that you will claim the serenity you need to carry you through the intense experiences of parenthood. I have learned you can always find serenity in the rain, in the snow, on the beach, under the tree, and even within the storm. Yes, even within the storm! Serenity can always be found in nature. Take a break in it when you are at your wit's end; walk, run, relax, and breathe in it. Send your children to the outdoors when you have pulled every last parenting trick from your sleeve and nothing feels as if it is working quite right. Spend time together in nature, learning from one another. Begin nurturing tasks by taking a breath in nature, even if it is from the window. And always remember: the slightest breeze blows in the wisest answers.

Special thanks to Kyra Ostendorf, my first editor. You continue to be a tremendous support to my mission. You are my favorite Saint Paul cheerleader and quickest-responding manager. Thank you once again for your expertise! I am grateful to Jean Cook for your editorial wisdom and guidance! Thank you for always directing me back to my best voice. To all the experts at Redleaf Press: Laurie Herrmann for all her help, guidance, and management; Eric Johnson; Laura Maki, who helped put the finishing sparkles on my books. A special appreciation goes to the acquisitions committee, David Heath, Inga Weberg, and Joanne Voltz, and publisher Linda Hein, for supporting my goal to help today's children.

Introduction

Raking in the Beauty

One year on the first day of spring, I gave my teenage son a rake to gather the old winter debris on our front lawn and my eight-year-old daughter a brown paper bag to pick up blown-down branches to use for kindling. While I pulled dead leaves from a flower bed and my son raked nearby, my daughter paused. Her eight-year-old mind turned profound, and she simply said, "This is a nice home." I looked at our home from my flower bed–level view, and I saw what she saw. Wow! Nature had done it again. It had brought the moment at hand to our eyes, to our fingertips, to all of our senses. As brief as this moment was, it touched my heart deeply. "This is the start of a new season—again," I thought to myself. "How perfect to work with my children in nature!" And I knew deep within that I wanted to share how powerfully nature has worked for me. I want to share it with you, and you can take what you like and apply it to your own life, your own classroom, your own philosophy.

Message from Nature

I started writing this book during a vacation to Ireland in the earliest part of spring. While sitting in a sunroom overlooking the sparkling bay of the western Dingle Peninsula, I noticed all the shades of green and recognized how nature alone can refresh my spirit. I looked at daffodils as though I were seeing them for the first time. I went for walks and took in the awesome beauty of the Cliffs of Moher, which towered more than six hundred feet above the bay. And I spent time looking at plants that exist only in this place. The word *miraculous* kept going through my mind. I found there were many answers and sometimes hidden and mysterious life messages within nature itself: "There is hope!" "Nothing is impossible!" "Keep growing!"

I want to offer my proactive approach to our fast-paced world, children's lack of time within nature, and their deficient personal connection with others. We need to continue to bring nature to children and to take children to nature. Doing so again and again is a fine antidote for our overstimulated children trying to make sense of our unbalanced world. My strategy includes developing an intrinsic respect for nature, discovering balance and wellness for ourselves, and extending this healthier lifestyle outward as we inspire others with our personal creativity. *Celebrate Nature!* is an integral part of this wholesome formula because nature restores, refreshes, and offers hope through its continually renewing process each and every season.

A Natural Design

The organization of this book plays off nature's consistent renewing process by following the natural cycle of the seasons. At its heart are four nature study sections: one each for autumn, winter, spring, and summer. Each nature study section includes seven themes that explore a type of animal, plant, process, or other subject associated with that time of year. No matter where you are in the school year, you can easily delve into the appropriate nature study section, select a theme, and begin anew, incorporating any of the ideas and activities into your curriculum.

Each nature study section opens with reflection: mine on that season's meaning for me, and yours, on memories of the season—tastes, smells, textures, images, traditions, and stories—to fill your spirit and your classroom. Next, I invite you to give the children a simple musical ritual for saying good-bye to the season they have just enjoyed and for welcoming the season ahead and all of its surprises. Following that, I offer suggestions for encouraging the children's families to participate as well.

Many of the lyrics I create for classroom use are sung to the simple tune of "Row, Row, Row Your Boat" or another familiar melody. I do this for two reasons. First, throughout the school year, the children can independently sing the songs. Second, the tune is consistent, and they can share their newfound songs at home, thus developing strong home-and-school connections.

Each season's seven themes open with suggestions for exploring outside. These ideas will help you provide the children with quality time outdoors, an opportunity for hands-on exploration, and the potential to become fascinated by an aspect of nature. In most cases, the field trips take you no farther than the school grounds and their neighborhood, but that act of simply enjoying nature is imperative and valuable. When you add dialogue with the children, you have quality beyond compare. If you choose to implement only one thing from this book, I encourage you to implement the Exploring Outside ideas and the sample questions, because respectfully witnessing nature's life is priceless. Doing so expands and fills the horizons of the young and curious minds in front of you.

Role play offers a fabulous way to strengthen both the social and intellectual skills of children. The Role Play Outside suggestions give children the chance to develop and use their language skills and confirm their new knowledge of nature firsthand. There are no props, just what nature provides—simply children using their imaginations outdoors. The role-play ideas are educationally sound when used alone—for instance, when there is limited quality time for being outdoors—but on the whole, the role-play suggestions are strongly reinforced when used with the Exploring Outside ideas.

A critical element in getting children into nature is bringing their families on board. Therefore, I include a section on involving families. When children can participate in family activities at home, the classroom nature study themes are reinforced. Getting families on board by encouraging them to have meaningful conversations in nature will add more health and wellness to their lives than we can imagine.

The Integrating Nature activities are the heart of each season's seven themes. These activities address science and discovery, math, blocks and building, language arts, reading, writing, dramatic play, art, and music, and they integrate nature into each areas of study. Let us take a look at one of the autumn themes—Fall Leaves. In the science and discovery area, provide magnifying glasses and a large bin full of leaves so the children can do close examination. In the math center, include rulers, strings, and other measuring devices, along with a surplus of leaves so the children can measure different sizes. Hang pictures of tree houses in the blocks center so the children can construct their own unique tree house with

Children are native explorers of green, mossy water sources, tadpole dwellings, and lichen growths. Watch as they uncover the earth's most interesting organic matter.

blocks. Guide the children as a large group in creating a haiku poem about fall leaves for language arts. Supply books about fall leaves for children to read in the reading center; encourage them to write about fall leaves in the writing center, and let them pretend to make fall-flavored pies with playdough in the dramatic play area. For art, the children can create artistic leaf prints and autumn-colored binoculars for viewing colorful leaves. And for music, they can sing songs about fall leaves. The nature themes are thoroughly integrated into each subject area, which strengthens the children's comprehension. Suggestions for open-ended questions are woven throughout the activities, and each theme ends with important questions to reinforce and strengthen students' comprehension. When nature is integrated into classroom study, when children interact in the natural world, and when their experiences at school and home connect, their learning is optimal.

I am grateful for readers like you, who care about our number one resource, children. I am thankful you want to make a difference by adding nature into their lives. The last chapter of *Celebrate Nature!* provides straightforward and down-to-earth ideas for integrating nature into your own life, as well as the children's.

Celebrate Nature

There will always be a space for nature in life's classroom. It will appear spontaneously when the teacher and the student are ready. When it presents itself to you, take hold of that moment and use it as your jumping-off point, just as I did when my daughter looked at our home from our front yard's flower bed. "This is a nice home" will become a profound learning mantra for both you and your students. Nature's classroom provides more than the basic academics; it presents reflection and nurture both inside and outside the classroom. I hope *Celebrate Nature!* helps you celebrate all of nature's offerings and the children in your care.

Returning to the Child's Garden

Two stories come to my mind that paint a better picture than any list of reasons (rising rates of childhood obesity, excessive use of overstimulating electronics and got-to-have-it gadgets, massive amounts of television time, and violent video games, to name a few) I could devise about why children need nature. These stories illustrate why children need nature, what they can learn from it, and how we can help them return to nature and celebrate it.

Losing It

I work in an elementary school that educates pre-K through sixth-grade students. Therefore, the faculty in my school work with students ranging from as young as three years old to as old as thirteen. Our faculty meetings encompass the global concerns of our educational community. In preparation for a faculty meeting, the principal sent everyone an agenda. All the typical topics were listed, and I anticipated discussion about one: electronic devices. To initiate the discussion, the principal reminded us that our school's policy was that students could not use electronic devices, such as video gaming devices, cell phones, and other distracting electronic handheld gadgets, while at school. Then she suggested we review that policy.

Because children had long bus rides to school (heaven forbid that they simply visit or play sign, color, or car games on the way to school), the bus drivers had begun to tolerate the use of electronic devices. These probably made the drivers' jobs easier, because the children sat quietly while using them. But these electronic devices, especially handheld video games and text-messaging cell phones, had made it into school, and although the school's policy stated otherwise, many of the children were playing with these electronics during recess. Like the bus drivers, many of the playground monitors appreciated the children's use of electronic games during recess because they made the monitors' jobs easier. They talked about how some of the more difficult children were not getting into trouble as much. Because these children were not arguing or fighting with others, many of the monitors preferred to let them use their electronic devices on the playground.

I couldn't believe how many school employees wanted to allow these devices at school! The discussion's tone was so serious that I seriously lost it! I found myself bursting at the seams, laughing. In fact, I could hardly breathe I was laughing so hard. Bless my principal—she looked around at my colleagues sitting at tables nearby and assumed they were making me laugh. I simply could not believe we were considering allowing children to go down this path, even if it might be detrimental to them.

Eventually I composed myself well enough to mimic, "Oh, let's not teach the children to use their words." I laughed some more as I pretended to be a playground monitor. Pointing to a colleague whom I put in the role of the difficult child, I said, "You can't get along with others, so go sit on the bench and play with your electronic device." At this point, others began to join me in my laughter. They too agreed that changing the policy was not in the best interest of the children, even though it made our jobs easier. Sometimes children's behavior is what it takes to remind teachers what to do.

Summer Year-Round

If I had to choose which season most influences my attitude, it would be summer. For teachers, summer is the time to forget progress reports, training sessions, anecdotal records, and benchmarks. It is a breakaway, time to relax and enjoy what is in front of us. I often wonder why I can't seem to keep my summer attitude during all the seasons.

I think one reason I love to teach young children so very much is because they have the summer attitude going all the time. They know how to be in the moment and always look at the life in front of them.

One time while doing a lesson on numbers and number writing, I had all my fancy-shmansy doohickey teaching tools ready. I had my sandpaper-textured numerals and my math manipulatives at my fingertips. I was *so* prepared. It was a hot day, and for the most part, I had the children's attention—that is, until smack-dab in the middle of my lesson, a small, strange-looking beetle crawled across the floor. It took only one child to shout, "Hey, look at the bug!" to cause us all to lose it. We lost our focus on my well-prepared lesson. Or maybe we just transferred it.

In a moment of summer attitude, I threw aside all my prepared materials and went with the children's attention. I caught the beetle in an insect container. We counted its legs. We then practiced writing *six* in the air. We decided to let it go and went outside. Once outdoors, we took ten giant steps to the big tree. We counted the nineteen seconds it took the beetle to fly out of the jar. Then we found eight more bugs on the playground (seven of which were insects and one a spider). Once back indoors, I was able to use all the number jargon from our "Hey, look at the bug!" adventure as my starting point. I did my number lesson, but I used the children's excitement and interests to direct the lesson. All this occurred because children love life—they love its fullness. Time and again, my students teach me to enjoy the moment in front of me. And nature has an effortless way of teaching us how to celebrate life: just watch a bug do its natural agenda for more than two minutes, or follow the course of a bud to blossom, and you will see this celebration at its optimum.

Growing Up Low-Tech

Life seems so different for children now. When I grew up in the '70s and '80s, nature was our dwelling from after school until nearly sundown. We made forts in it and hid among evergreens. Underneath the trees, we wrote messages in the dirt and made paths in the dried pine needles. We occupied ourselves by setting up our outside kids-only abode. We played King of the Hill, and our jeans were grass stained and our fingernails were dirty. We used stones for drawing and played hopscotch on sidewalks. We used sticks for bats and pebbles for balls (okay, so that wasn't such a good idea). Mostly we simply enjoyed the outdoors, our organic playground.

In our family, television was a special luxury. After adjusting our outdoor antenna to bring in one of three stations, the whole family watched a snowy picture of *Wild Kingdom* or *Little House on the Prairie*. Today television, handheld electronics, and computers are a way of life, and they consume children's time and energy. Interestingly enough, we have a record number of obese children and children on medications for short attention spans. I believe children's lack of time outdoors and their loads of time in front of television sets, computer games, and other electronic devices contribute to the problems they face.

According to Norman Herr, PhD, professor of science education at California State University, Northridge, 99 percent of American households have at least one television, and the average number of televisions in the average U.S. household is 2.24 (Herr 2010). Furthermore, 66 percent of Americans watch television while eating dinner. The most alarming of Herr's statistics is the number of minutes per week that parents spend in meaningful conversation with their children—3.5 minutes. *Only 3.5 minutes per week are spent in meaningful conversation.* At the same time, according to Herr, these same children are watching 1,680 minutes of television per week. Doctor John Nelson of the American Medical Association writes that with 2,888 of 3,000 studies showing that television and its influence contributes to real-life mayhem, "It's a public health problem" (Herr 2010). The American Psychiatric Association states, "We have had a long-standing concern with the impact of television on behavior, especially among children" (Herr 2010).

Broadcast news continually gives statistics and information regarding the topic of overstimulated children. While watching the WROC Rochester, New York, news one evening, I heard another disturbing statistic: one in ten young gamers shows signs of addiction. Their addictive behavior begins with lying about the number of hours they play games, skipping out on homework, and ceasing to do chores around the home. This alarmed me, because I've learned in my own training that one addiction may become a gateway to more problematic ones—for example, alcohol and drug abuse or eating disorders.

What has happened to children going outside simply to catch a breath of fresh air? What has happened to nature as a natural sedative and a calming effect in children's lives? I believe natural approaches and strategies can still help.

Hourglasses and Butterflies

Of course, we all experience technology and its many changes. At the school where I work, interactive whiteboards were installed in every teacher's classroom this year. The oversized computer boards, the newest got-to-have-it gadget for classrooms, are like monstrous computer touch screens for teachers and children to use. Although my computer skills are up to date, I find the whiteboards quite involved and could occupy my whole day learning this or that feature. I'm still getting used to actually writing with its interactive pen.

Once, while modeling for the children how to write a capital *M,* I found the nub on the whiteboard's pen didn't quite catch the cursor, so my *M* looked like an alien symbol. I clicked on the eraser gizmo in the software toolbox and tried to erase the *M* to start over. My computer froze, and I couldn't do anything until the hourglass icon disappeared. I attempted to explain this to my classroom of seventeen three- and four-year-olds, saying, "Boys and girls, we are waiting for the hourglass to unfreeze." I pointed to it, and the children numbly gazed. My adult mind thought this was all quite entertaining, but one child blurted out, "Can we play?"

When the computer thawed, I worked swiftly to get the children's attention back, and as a class we spent a considerable amount of time clicking and dragging pieces on the whiteboard to put together a monarch butterfly puzzle. We got through it, and when the puzzle was complete, everyone cheered as if we'd won some special techy triathlon.

Later I considered pulling the old low-tech butterfly floor puzzle out of a cupboard, and I wondered how many children do actual puzzles anymore—the ones with genuine puzzle pieces you physically touch. Instead, I decided to take the children outside to look for real butterflies, and they cheered even louder when I announced my plan.

When I as the teacher feel the heaviness and exhaustion from this unbelievably demanding occupation and wonder how I can continue any longer, I take the kids outside into nature, and we sit in the sunlight. From this space, I can think about how to do it better. We all need this type of rejuvenation, especially children. There is always a moment outdoors when a child I can't quite reach in the classroom brings a leaf over to me and says, "Look at this green worm!" We look at the green worm together, and we connect. These are the teaching moments I cherish, and when they occur, I know in my heart that I have done the perfect thing: I have brought the children to the outdoors, to their organic playground of innate learning and creative energy. It's the place where they come to me and question everything under the sun and experience life itself. From this hands-on, real space, I feel like I *can* go on for the next twenty-five years (all right—maybe only twenty years) as a teacher. Nature always has a way of doing just that, refreshing the spirit.

Getting Unplugged

We need a healthy balance between working with technology, being plugged into information 24/7, and experiencing the permanent renewal that nature provides. Research supports what others and I know in our hearts: that children truly benefit from simply enjoying quality time outdoors every day. In a study of children aged five to eighteen, researchers from the University of Illinois at Urbana-Champaign demonstrated that attention deficit hyperactivity disorder (ADHD) symptoms are significantly reduced when the children spend quality time outdoors enjoying nature (Hogan 2004). (I took note that the study referred to *quality* time outdoors: it didn't discuss texting, playing handheld video games, or fidgeting with other electronic gadgets while in nature.)

Most important, I believe, is that many people are beginning to see the need to do research about children and nature. More and more researchers want to prove with scientifically defensible data that children can be helped in many ways simply by going outside. These scientific studies will undoubtedly confirm what we nature enthusiasts already know about the effects of nature and its miraculous antidotes. Giving children doses of time on green grass, in fresh air—all the life and energy nature has to offer the mind—is wonderful.

Times change and gadgets upgrade, but nature is always there. Nature is always changing, too, which is part of its beauty and another reason we can learn so much from it. With this aim and more, you'll find the next four chapters—Autumn, Winter, Spring, and Summer Nature Studies—chock-full of ideas and activities. Use as many of these as you wish—or all of them—to integrate nature's wonder into your lessons. Create a child's garden in your very own classroom!

References

Herr, Norman. 2010. "Television and Health." Internet Resources to Accompany *The Sourcesbook for Teaching Science*. www.csun.edu/science/health/docs/tv&health.html#tv_stats.

———. 2010. "Television and Health." Internet Resources to Accompany *The Sourcesbook for Teaching Science*. Dr. John Nelson quote found at www.csun.edu/science/health/docs/tv&health.html#influence.

———. 2010. "Television and Health." Internet Resources to Accompany *The Sourcesbook for Teaching Science*. American Psychiatric Association quote found at www.csun.edu/science/health/docs/tv&health.html#influence.

Hogan, Dan. 2004. "Children with ADHD Benefit from Time Outdoors Enjoying Nature." www.sciencedaily.com/releases/2004/08/040830082535.htm.

Autumn Nature Study
September, October, November

Autumn Reading List

Here is a list of the books I recommend providing to children throughout the autumn themes:

Carle, Eric. *The Very Busy Spider.*
———. *The Very Hungry Caterpillar.*
Ehlert, Lois. *Leaf Man.*
———. *Red Leaf, Yellow Leaf.*
Gibbons, Gail. *Apples.*
———. *Monarch Butterfly.*
———. *Spiders.*
Graham, Margaret Bloom. *Be Nice to Spiders.*
Hall, Zoe. *The Apple Pie Tree.*
Law, Felicia. *The Feathers.*
Potter, Beatrix. *The Tale of Squirrel Nutkin.*
Rabe, Tish. *Fine Feathered Friends: All About Birds.*
Titherington, Jeanne. *Pumpkin Pumpkin.*
Watt, Melanie. *Scaredy Squirrel.*
Williams, Linda. *The Little Old Lady Who Was Not Afraid of Anything.*

Embracing Changes and Migration

Regardless of where we live in the northern hemisphere—Southern California, New York, China, or Ireland—we cannot deny the season of autumn. In some areas of the world, its changes may be subtler than in others. Regardless, autumn exists in some form everywhere. Autumn is the season of examining change. I believe teachers are the ones to spot autumn first. They sniff out even the slightest tinge of the fall season. Many of us sense the end of summer approaching as we hear the sound of geese overhead and notice the slightest change in leaf color. Once autumn looms at our back door and we prepare for the upcoming school year, we are ready to help playful children notice all the changes of this picturesque season. We become their first teachers of many new experiences, and autumn is a beautiful time of the year to begin our important work.

My Autumn Reflection

When I was younger, I treasured autumn and all of its wonder, especially on Saturdays. All weekend we raked leaves and gathered them alongside the ditches. We found autumn games to play once our task of raking was exhausted.

For example, my friend would cover me completely in leaves and then run to find other nearby neighborhood kids to ask if they would help find me. I would lie still under the colorful foliage, and then she would cleverly lead them near the pile. I would hear her say, "We were playing here, and then she was gone." When it seemed as if they might be buying her story, I would roar and reach my arms straight out from the pile, as though I were Frankenstein's monster awakening. I would grab their ankles. They would quickly realize that the stunt was another one of our kids-only scare tactics, and we would set out to find other kid things to do with leaves and the autumn air.

We did this because of our parents' "Go rake the leaves" plot. You see, our raking job never was truly finished, because the leaves kept falling. I realized later in life that raking leaves is a parents' conspiracy to keep children outdoors and busy in nature! As kids, we were absolutely present in our outdoor activities, something many of today's children struggle with. Somehow, once our parents made us go outdoors, we were simply part of nature, just like the fresh air and the falling leaves. Nature enhanced our minds, allowing us to be full of spontaneity and creative play, both of which are beneficial to children.

Your Autumn Reflection

Autumn is the transition from summer to winter, the change from hot to cold. What has autumn meant to you? Perhaps you grew up observing the autumn grain turning golden and being harvested. Maybe you watched autumn emerge growing up near the ocean, noticing the sky and water transform with the oncoming season. Maybe you recall falling leaves, pumpkin carving, dunking for apples, and eating everything apple under the sun: applesauce, apple butter, apple cider, apple pie, apple crisp, apples galore! Which autumn memories come to mind for you? Which ones can you share with your students? Storytelling that includes brilliant seasonal attributes is a good way to bring nature to children's minds, and it can inspire them to get outdoors on their unstructured Saturdays to create their own stories.

Autumn is here! Let's get right into the season and the fun weeks ahead. Use the teacher reflection that follows as a beginning point, a place to breathe in nature and take in the healthiness of the autumn season. I always find using a balancing tool such as this a good space to begin from before heading into the challenging world of teaching little ones.

What does autumn mean to you?

_____

_____

_____

_____

_____

_____

What has this season meant to you in the past?

_____

_____

_____

_____

_____

_____

What autumn stories come to your mind?

_____

_____

_____

_____

_____

How will you personally take time to enjoy this particular season?

_____

_____

_____

_____

_____

What are you thankful for this autumn season?

_____

_____

_____

_____

_____

How will you set the tone for the season ahead?

_____

_____

_____

_____

Are there any special activities you can include to bring in the season in your unique way?

_____

_____

_____

_____

_____

Sing in the Season

Give the children a simple musical ritual for saying good-bye to the season they have just enjoyed and welcoming the season ahead with all of its surprises. Practicing this ritual also provides a healthy sense of saying good-bye, letting go, and surrendering to what is in front of us. Begin the season with this simple song: "Good-bye, Summer! Hello, Autumn!" Sing it to the tune of "Good Night, Ladies":

Good-bye, Summer! Hello, Autumn!
Good-bye, summer; good-bye, summer; good-bye, summer;
We enjoyed you so!

Hello, autumn; hello, autumn; hello, autumn;
We welcome you right now!

Invite Families to Participate

Encourage families to join their children in noticing autumn and examining change. Send home a brief introductory letter to families to introduce your upcoming nature activities for autumn. Remember—you are helping out tremendously by including families in your getting-children-outdoors mission and wholesome environment education. Ask families to provide either a fall picture or some other type of autumn sign, such as leaves, apples, acorns, gourds or small pumpkins, feathers, or anything else that will bring the autumn topic to curious young minds. Here is a sample letter to send home:

Dear Families,

Happy almost autumn! As we prepare for the upcoming fall season in our classroom, we will be asking for your help in the weeks ahead. The children will soon be delving into these autumn topics at school:

- Fall Leaves
- Monarch Butterflies
- Autumn's Apples
- Perfect Pumpkins
- Spider Species
- Searching for Squirrels
- Flying Feathers

Be on the lookout this fall for our simple nature homework activities. These will all be wholesome, fun family activities that will provide enjoyment for the season, such as taking a walk in nature and observing squirrels, trees, and other autumn attributes.

In the meantime, please send a simple autumn treasure with your child to school. We will add it to our Autumn Family Treasures box. Items can include such things as a picture of a fun family autumn activity or special leaves, acorns, or feathers you have found during the fall season. We will be discussing all of the items during our group circle time. Our group time discussions will enhance the children's listening, speaking, reading, and writing skills and provide an opportunity to integrate the seasonal theme into all their learning.

Thank you in advance for all of your autumn contributions. More important, thank you for your involvement with your child's education! Children need plenty of time outdoors enjoying nature. They need time to appreciate the simple things our environment has to offer. I value having you join me in helping with this important task.

Here's to celebrating the autumn season and all of its gifts.

My best to you,
[insert your signature]

Decorate a shoe box or other box with construction paper in autumn colors. Be as creative as you wish. Label the box "Autumn Family Treasures." When they bring their treasure items to school, have the children put the items in the autumn treasure chest. Later let each child share about the original items during your group meeting time.

In your weekly newsletters, remind families of specific requests during this season, such as discussing the importance of trees or sending in a sign of autumn, such as a pretty leaf, an apple, or a small pumpkin. In the newsletter, also mention the upcoming optional home activities created to help families and their children connect with nature and all its richness.

Christine shares a story about the feather she found while on a nature walk with her family.

Autumn Theme 1: Fall Leaves

Exploring Outside

Take children on a nature hike. Before you go, everyone in the group can make binoculars (see Art activity, page 23) to use on the hike. Allow the children to view leaves through the binoculars. Ask open-ended questions throughout your walk. Questions such as "What do the leaves look like?" will help children to examine autumn's characteristics more closely. Point out characteristics and ask other questions, such as these:

What colors do you see in the
    trees?
Why are the leaves turning colors?
What do the leaves sound like in
    the wind?
What do they look like when they
    fall?
Do they make sounds when they
    fall? What sounds?
What else do you notice?

Easily created binoculars help children feel like great explorers of the outdoors.

Role Play Outside

While outdoors, explain to the children that they get to be leaves. Ask them to move and dance like falling leaves. Join in the fun as you, the teacher, become the autumn wind. Children should use "I" terms when actually pretending to be the leaves—for example, "I am a red leaf" or "I am falling off a tree." Begin by asking, "What do you look like?" The potential questions are endless. Be sure to once again ask open-ended questions. This helps children to develop higher-level thinking skills. Here are some fine examples of open-ended questions:

What do you look like?
Why are you falling?
What do you like about yourself?
What is happening to you?

Involving Families: Studying Leaves at Home

Supply the children with some fun activities to do at home. Mention the activities in your weekly newsletter to families. Explain to families that these optional activities are provided for extra quality time together in nature and for involvement in their children's education. Explain that this season the children are learning about a precious resource called trees. Describe the following nature activities for the families to enjoy at home:

Give the children plenty of time to practice being leaves, dancing like leaves in the wind and becoming part of the season at hand.

- Ask parents to send in five special leaves they find on an autumn outing with their child. Tell them to send their leaves to school in a resealable plastic bag. Later you can include all the leaves in a large bin for observing in the classroom, or they can be included as part of a leaf crunch table.

- Ask parents to discuss the importance of trees. Ask them to describe how trees help in providing birds and other animals shelter. Trees also provide us with shade and oxygen.

- Ask families to play outside, taking time specifically to look at leaves, their veins, and their connections to the branches and to the tree.

- Suggest raking or pushing together a collection of leaves. After having fun jumping, rolling, and playing in the leaves, look at the leaves individually and consider how some of them look similar to or different from others.

Integrating Nature: Studying Fall Leaves in the Classroom

Have each child bring a bag of autumn leaves back to the classroom. Keep the bags in a separate area. You will be using the leaves in many of the following fall leaf activities in the areas of science and discovery, math, blocks and building, language arts, reading, writing, dramatic play, art, and music.

Science and Discovery

- In a table or large bin, allow a small group of children to explore leaves. Provide magnifying glasses for more scientific discovery.

- Encourage children to draw a picture of what they did while exploring leaves in the discovery area. When you ask what they've drawn, write the children's verbal responses alongside their drawings. Certainly it is advisable to ask open-ended questions about any pictures the children did not explain thoroughly. Simply point to a picture and say, "Tell me more about this" or "Can you share more about this?"

- Provide color paddles for children to look through as they discover the leaves and examine the autumn colors.

- After leaves dry in the table or large bin, let it become a leaf crunch table. As they crunch the leaves into tinier pieces, the children can discuss the different sounds and textures leaves create.

Math

- Include various sizes of leaves for independent comparing and estimation. Give the children measurement tools, such as rulers and lengths of string. Ask children what they notice about the different-sized leaves.

- Model for children how to make a pattern using leaves that are small and large or have other characteristics. Examples might be small, large, small, large, and pointy, round, pointy, round. Use any leaf characteristics in creating an individual autumn pattern.

- Allow the children to sort through tubs that include math items in various colors. Focus on the sorting of autumn colors, such as red, yellow, orange, and brown. Model for the children how to sort autumn colors from other colors.

Teacher Reminder:
Having children decipher color and other characteristics is a fine early math skill to offer in the math center.

Blocks and Building

- Turn your block and building area into a tree house construction area. Find pictures of different tree house designs on the Internet, print them, and hang them for viewing in your blocks center. Talk about how autumn is a fine time of year to be in a tree house. Let your construction crew develop its own tree house designs. This will be a favorite center for the children to return to in your upcoming Autumn's Apples theme (see page 37).

Language Arts

- As a large group, create a nature haiku poem titled "Fall Leaves." Haiku poems are beautiful for teaching things about nature. A haiku poem uses a simple format: a seventeen-syllable verse form that consists of three lines of five, seven, and five syllables. Each haiku usually contains a *kigo,* a word that indicates in which season the poem takes place.

  It isn't always easy to decipher in what season the poem takes place. However, for all practical purposes, *snow* suggests winter, *buds* or *blossoms* suggest spring, and *sun* or *insects* suggest summer.

  Here is a simple format I use for creating a haiku poem:

  First line = five syllables including the *kigo* word to decipher the season
  Second line = seven syllables describing and addressing the title
  Third line = five syllables finishing the haiku poem

  And here is an example of a haiku:

  Fall Leaves
  Leaves fall from the trees
  Colors amber, gold, and brown
  Trees for now say 'bye

  After completing a haiku, children can draw pictures about their leaf experiences outdoors to include with the poem.

Reading

- Provide nonfiction autumn books that depict the actual season and its attributes. Fiction that plays with the season will pique their interests as well. Some books you can feature include *Red Leaf, Yellow Leaf* and *Leaf Man*, both by Lois Ehlert.

Writing

- Include autumn-colored chunk crayons you buy or make from old crayons by melting old autumn-colored crayon bits in a muffin tin at 300 degrees Fahrenheit. Be sure to include leaves and paper with the crayons in the writing center. Then children can set a leaf under a blank piece of paper and rub the crayon on top to transfer the leaf's impression onto the paper.

- Provide sentence strips that include the word *leaves* and an autumn color. Including pictures to encourage emergent reading skills is helpful. Children can view and copy these strips. Allow the children to write and create at this literacy station. Example sentence strips can include sentences like these:

  Leaves turn brown and fall from trees.
  Leaves turn yellow and fall from trees.
  Leaves turn orange and fall from trees.
  Leaves turn red and fall from trees.

On the sentence strips, highlight the color words *red, yellow, orange,* and *brown,* using corresponding colored markers or pens to encourage the children's early word recognition. The words *leaves* and *trees* can be copied in green. These literacy gestures help with word recognition and one-to-one reading correspondence.

Children aged three, four, and five can practice becoming strong writers. Include predictable sentence strips for the children to dictate from, which will strengthen their early writing abilities at the foundation of learning.

Dramatic Play

- In your dramatic play area, let the children become pastry chefs while pretending to bake autumn-flavored pies, such as apple, pumpkin, and forest berry. Include playdough and a basket of wooden toy rolling pins, plastic knives, craft sticks, and some cookie cutters. Bring in aprons, pot holders, and recyclable aluminum pie plates. If you have it, introduce play food, such as artificial fruit and imitation pie slices. The children will enjoy rolling out the dough and creating a pie for you to sample. Tell them they are superb pastry chefs.

    You can use this center in your upcoming Autumn's Apples (page 38) and Perfect Pumpkins (page 46) themes too.

Art

- Using autumn colors of tempera paint (red, yellow, orange, and brown), allow the children to make leaf prints. Model how to lightly paint the leaves, textured-side up, making sure to cover every area of their stem, veins, and surface. Lift up the leaf and press the painted leaf down onto white construction paper. By putting a paper towel over the top of the leaf and gently using a circular motion with your fingertips, you will be able to include on your print every vein of the leaf. Show the children what happens when you overlap two leaves and two colors, such as red and yellow, to create orange. Let them discover the blending of autumn colors to create new colors.

Children will wear their autumn binoculars just like nature explorers do. Trentyn and Brionna paint their binoculars red.

- Create autumn binoculars. Staple together two toilet paper tissue holders and let the children paint the homemade binoculars with autumn colors. After they dry, punch holes in the side and tie them together with autumn-colored string (such as red, orange, or yellow). Tell the children you are going to go on an autumn foliage walk and will be looking specifically for autumn colors and autumn leaves. Use these binoculars for the nature hike that opens this Fall Leaves theme (page 18).

Children capture the feel of a tree's bark in their rubbings.

- Make tree bark rubbings using construction paper and old brown, black, and gray crayons. Show the children how to place the paper on the trunk of the tree, and using the side of the crayon against the paper, make textured tree bark prints.

Music

- Sing "Fall Leaves" to the tune of "This Old Man."

Fall Leaves
Autumn leaves,
Falling down,
I love to watch the leaves fall
    down.
All the red, yellow, brown,
    orange, and gold—
The autumn leaves are falling
    down.

Closing the Fall Leaves Theme

Throughout your work with the Fall Leaves activities, ask children questions that further enhance their comprehension and appreciation. In your group times, be sure to discuss why trees are important. Here are some additional questions you can use during activities to bring this theme to a close.

Why do leaves turn colors?
What do trees give us?
What do trees give other animals?

Autumn Theme 2: Monarch Butterflies

Exploring Outside

Before heading outside to look for monarch butterflies in early autumn, teach children about the midstage creatures as caterpillars that eventually become adult insects. Explain that although caterpillars look like creepy-crawly worms, some of them transform into beautiful insects like the monarch butterfly. Explain to the children that the monarch butterfly is a flying insect because it has a head, thorax (chest), abdomen, and six legs.

You will find monarch butterfly caterpillars on milkweed. Caterpillars that become monarch butterflies will feed on milkweed plants for nearly two weeks until they position themselves in a J shape on the underside of a leaf and cocoon themselves into their bright green and gold chrysalis. Bring along magnifying glasses for a closer look at these amazing creatures. Once you've found some, ask the children open-ended questions such as these:

Why do you think these caterpillars like milkweed?
Why do you think they hang upside down and form a J shape?
When do they know that it is time to become a butterfly?
How much do they eat?
Where do they go at night?
What else do you notice?

Abby, Trentyn, and Ethan examine a dead butterfly up close in the discovery center. By using a magnifying glass, they can compare and contrast the real butterfly with images from a book or magazine.

The potential for questions is endless. If you see actual monarch butterflies, use wonder statements like these to prompt the children into thinking and wondering too:

I wonder what they eat.
I wonder what they drink.
I wonder if they sleep.
I wonder where they live.

Role Play Outside

While outdoors, explain to the children that they get to be cater-pillars and then butterflies. Ask the children to move like a cat-erpillar and pretend to eat from the milkweed plant. Have them show you how to get inside their cocoon and sleep. While they are in their cocoons, ask them to change, to transform, to metamor-phose into monarch butterflies. When answering your questions, children should use "I" terms while pretending to be a caterpil-lar or butterfly, such as "Look at me! I changed into a monarch butterfly." Asking open-ended questions gives children the chance to strengthen their language skills and expand their thought pro-cesses. Here are some questions you can use:

What do you look like?
How do you feel?
What do you do?
What is the best thing about being you?

Involving Families: Studying Butterflies at Home

Supply the children with some fun activities to do at home. Mention the activities in your weekly newsletter to families. Explain to fami-lies that the optional activities are provided for extra quality time together in nature and for involvement in their children's educa-tion. Explain that the children are learning about the term *metamor-phosis* and about a beautiful insect, the monarch butterfly. Describe the following nature activities for the families to enjoy at home:

- In the early autumn, ask families to go on monarch butterfly exploration walks with their children. They can also be on the lookout for caterpillars and chrysalises. Send home a half sheet of paper with this question written on it: "Did you see a monarch butterfly on your autumn walk?" Be sure to include yes and no check boxes on the paper. Provide a line at the top for the child to sign his or her name, which is another great skill to practice at home and will help you recognize which families have sent these papers back to school. Tell families that you will be creating a classroom graph with the returned papers, and you will appreciate their filling out the enclosed half sheets with their yes or no responses. After the papers have been returned to school, create a graph on your chart paper and discuss the graph terms and phrases *most, least, how many more than, how many less than,* and *equal to* (see the math activity, page 28).

- Tell families that their children are also learning about fiction and make-believe. Ask for parents' help in making your academic lessons come alive by sending in a make-believe costume for your dramatic play area. The children will take turns metamorphosing or transforming into different creatures. Oftentimes during autumn, many parents have old Halloween costumes on hand. Any make-believe dress-up item will do: a cat, giraffe, or other animal costume. Certainly a pumpkin or other food-related costume would offer a fun transformation as well (see dramatic play, page 31).

Integrating Nature: Studying Monarch Butterflies in the Classroom

Bring a few caterpillars back to the classroom from your Exploring Outside trek. Remember—do not forget to bring the milkweed plants too! I cut the plants and insert them into water vases for a longer life, because the caterpillars do not like to eat wilted old milkweed. You can cut more every few days to bring in food for them until they form their chrysalises. Remind the children that once the caterpillars transform to butterflies, you will be setting them free for their migration. In addition to checking on the caterpillars daily, the children will study monarch butterflies in the science and discovery, math, blocks and building, language arts, reading, writing, dramatic play, art, and music activities that follow.

Science and Discovery

- Include posters of monarch butterflies and their life cycle in your science area. Enhance the student's learning by including labels and interesting information. For example, include a picture of a caterpillar hanging in its J formation just before it spins its chrysalis. The picture's caption could read, "The caterpillar is getting ready to spin its chrysalis." A language-rich science and discovery area helps develop children's literacy skills too.

On the way outdoors to look for monarch butterflies, the children spotted these little caterpillars searching for milkweed plants. I was amazed by how long they wanted to observe and look intently at the brightly striped crawling creatures.

- If possible, find some caterpillars already in their chrysalises. Caterpillars usually create chrysalises on milkweed plants toward the end of summer. Cut the milkweed with the attached chrysalis, bring it into the classroom, and insert it into a clear jar with holes for oxygen or a mesh net holder specifically used for hatching butterflies. Be sure to include flowers in water, because monarch chrysalises usually hatch within eight to twelve days. If the butterfly hatches over a weekend while everyone is at home, it will have the nectar from the flowers to survive on until you return to school. Once you're back, name the newly hatched butterfly and release it in nature.

- If your milkweed and chrysalis hunt has left you empty-handed, you can order monarch butterflies from an educational supplies catalog. They will arrive as miniature caterpillars and eventually metamorphose to form their chrysalises and then their beautiful butterfly form. Make sure the kit includes fresh milkweed to feed them.

Math

- During your group time, discuss the children's autumn walks with their families. Create a math graph from the information families returned on the papers you sent them asking "Did you see a monarch butterfly on your autumn walk?" Title your chart paper "Did you see a monarch butterfly on your autumn walk?" Then add *Yes* and *No* columns, and include all the families' responses. Tape the families' papers to the chart paper in the correct column. Then discuss the graph terms *most, least, how many more than, how many less than,* and *equal to* in relation to the results on the graph.

Blocks and Building

- During the monarch butterflies theme, transform your blocks and building center into a large-motor skill and literacy area. Introduce letter development by modeling for the children how to spell the word *butterfly* with various curved and straight blocks. Begin by typing and printing out a poster in a simple block font spelling out the word *butterfly*. Include pictures of butterflies all around the poster and place it on a wall in your block area.

  Next, show the children the poster and suggest they copy the word *butterfly* using the blocks. Show them how to use curved blocks for making curvy letters, such as *b* and *e,* and how to use straight blocks for making straight letters, such as *t* and *y*. If you have a bucket of plastic butterflies for the children to place on top of the block word, great. If not, print out colored pictures of butterflies for the children to place alongside their butterfly words. Ask the children, "What do all those letters spell?" As they independently practice, praise them as you comment, "Wow, you spelled the word *butterfly* using blocks and butterflies. Great spelling!" Use this block and building idea in your Summer's Insects (page 187), Busy Honeybees (page 215), and Picnic Ants (pages 221–22) themes as well.

Language Arts

- Teach children about writing fiction. Ask them if they enjoy daydreaming and using their imagination. Mention that the other day you thought it would be fun and creative to pretend to change into something. Talk about *metamorphosis,* as when the caterpillar transforms into a butterfly. Ask all the children to share what they would like to change into. Some may say a kitty cat, others a giraffe, and some a race car. Next, teach the children in uncomplicated terms the difference between nonfiction and fiction. Explain to the children that although they enjoy imagining things, they really cannot change into a giraffe or race car. Changing into these things is make-believe. Simply put, fiction is make-believe, and nonfiction is true or factual. Fiction is meant to entertain. Nonfiction provides facts, informs the reader, and may of course entertain too.

- Create a fiction book together called *Transforming: If I Could Transform into Anything, I Would Become _____!* Ask the children what they would transform into and record all their responses on chart paper. Then have them draw their responses on a sheet printed with the sentence, "If I could transform into anything,

I would become _____!" For younger children, write their responses on the blank line. For more advanced learners, help them record their own responses. Older children can phonetically sound out and write their responses independently. Put all the pages together for a classroom big book. Read it to the class and put it in your reading center for more independent reading time. The children will enjoy reading their *Transforming* book again and again.

Reading

- Provide various caterpillar and butterfly books in your reading center for children to explore. Books on luna moths and other moths will be an interesting connection too. Make available various nonfiction books that depict a butterfly's body parts. This will be great for your curious children. Fiction books should be provided as well. Some books you can feature include *Monarch Butterfly* by Gail Gibbons and *The Very Hungry Caterpillar* by Eric Carle.

Writing

- Tape a sentence strip in the writing center that reads, "I can read about the life cycle of the monarch butterfly." Include several pictures with captions about the life cycle of the butterfly. You can draw simple pictures by hand or obtain some from free sites on the Internet. Here are some simple captions for each picture:

  The monarch butterfly lays its eggs on milkweed.
  A baby monarch caterpillar hatches from the egg.
  The caterpillar eats milkweed leaves.
  The caterpillar begins to pupate. The caterpillar hangs
       upsidedown and forms a J shape.
  The caterpillar forms a chrysalis.
  A monarch butterfly emerges from the chrysalis.

  Be sure to number these life cycle picture cards on the back. The children can then independently put these in order.

- Provide the children with blank paper and colored pencils and crayons to create their own writing and illustrations from the life cycle pictures and captions. Allow them to practice their writing independently. While working in this center with children, prompt them by asking which life cycle pictures they will be creating today.

Dramatic Play

- Autumn is the perfect time of year to include costumes in your dramatic play center. Use the costumes and dress-up items that families have sent to school at your request. Include a sheet on your dramatic play mirror that reads, "Look at me! I transformed into a _____." During independent center play, when the children choose what they want to transform into, read the message on the mirror to the children and ask them to fill in the blank by communicating what they have dressed up as and changed into.

Art

- Teach the children about symmetrical art. In simple terms, when thinking of symmetrical art and explaining it to children, talk about looking in the mirror and seeing a mirror image. A simple art activity using symmetry can be done by creating abstract artistic butterflies.

Catrice smiles as her teacher helps unfold her artistic symmetrical butterfly.

Copy an abstract butterfly shape onto 12 x 18 inch white construction paper, making sure the sides are symmetrical. Have the children cut out the shape and then fold the paper in half. Open up the paper butterfly as if it were a greeting card. Using a small paintbrush and tempera paints, have the children place ten small dots of assorted colors on only one side of the paper. Count the dots together. Then fold the paper in half again and smooth it to press the paint onto the opposite side. Unfold the paper together as you say in amazement, "Wow! Look at the symmetry." Once the paint is dry, provide a black construction paper circle for the head and two black oval shapes for the thorax and abdomen. Supply two small black strips for some curly antennae too. Give the children glue sticks to add antennae that they can curl with their fingers and white crayons to add eyes.

- Provide mirrors at the art center to use with the butterfly creations. After children open their creations, model for them how to place a mirror in the center of the artwork and view their symmetrical design this way. Remove the mirror to view their actual artwork. Ask the children to define symmetry.

Music

- Sing "Monarch Butterfly" to the tune of "Frère Jacques":

  Monarch Butterfly
  Monarch butterfly, monarch butterfly,
  Migrating south, migrating south.
  How long will it take you?
  How long will it take you?
  To migrate south? To migrate south?

  After singing, ask the children to predict how long it will take the monarch butterfly to migrate south.

Closing the Monarch Butterflies Theme

Throughout your Monarch Butterflies activities, ask children questions that further enhance their comprehension and appreciation. In your group times, be sure to discuss interesting facts about the monarch butterflies. Include their color, the fact that they are migratory insects, and their life cycle. Here are some additional questions you can use to bring this theme to a close:

  What do you find interesting about monarch butterflies?
  What have you learned about monarch butterflies?
  What else would you like to tell us about monarch butterflies?

Autumn Theme 3: Autumn's Apples

Exploring Outside

If you are lucky enough to have apple trees on school grounds, take the children outdoors to observe some of nature's finest apple trees. Or contact a local apple orchard and take the children on an Autumn's Apples field trip.

If a field trip is out the question, walk to a farmers' market where apples, pumpkins, and other produce are sold. A grocery store will do as well. The children will treasure the experience for a lifetime. Be sure to take many pictures for use during other apple integration activities in the classroom.

Throughout your tour, ask open-ended questions such as these to help children to tune into the fruit farm and all its offerings more closely:

What do you notice?
How do you get the apples down?
How long do you think it takes an apple to grow ripe?
How do the apples get to the store?
What else do you notice?

Teacher Reminder:
You can connect the next two autumn activities, Autumn's Apples and Perfect Pumpkins (page 41), by finding an apple- and pumpkin-picking farm where you can take your class.

Role Play Outside

While outdoors, explain to the children they can be autumn's apples. Ask the children to say what color apple they are. Statements such as "Tell me about yourself!" always create a fine opening and generate imaginative dialogue. Ask the children to use "I" statements—for example, "I am a juicy red apple hanging on the tree." All this helps with identification and language skills.

Continue using open-ended questions to help develop the children's higher-level thinking:

What do people love about you and other apples?
How long did it take you to grow?
What do you look like?
How did you get here?
What do you like about yourself?
Where are you going *(the store, someone's home . . .)*?

Involving Families: Studying Apples at Home

Supply the children with some fun activities to do at home. Mention the activities in your weekly newsletter to families. Explain to families that the optional activities are provided for extra quality time together in nature and for involvement in their children's education. Explain that the children are learning about one of nature's perfect foods, apples. Describe the following nature activities for the families to enjoy at home:

- Ask families to send two apples with their child to school if possible. Tell them you look forward to all the varieties that show up. You will be using the apples to have a taste test and to make applesauce. Tell them you appreciate their contribution to your academic lesson. Tell them that the children will be learning about measuring, preparing food, and creating their own recipe (see the Math activity, page 36, and the Science and Discovery activity, pages 35–36).

- Invite families to conduct their own taste test at home.

- Share the apple sauce recipe with families so they can make this treat too.

Integrating Nature: Studying Apples in the Classroom

Bring several varieties of apples to the classroom for more investigative learning. To expand children's comprehension, also bring other apple items, such as apple cider, apple juice, apple pie, applesauce, and apple butter. If your classroom budget is an issue, ask families to donate some apple items for your upcoming apple theme. Explain that they will be used in science and discovery, math, blocks, language arts, reading, writing, dramatic play, art, and music activities.

Science and Discovery

- Include large pictures or posters of apples in your discovery area. Be sure to include a colorful life cycle picture of an apple as well.

- Near the apple pictures, put a place card that says, "Items made from apples." Next to it, set items made from apples that do not have to be immediately refrigerated, such as unopened apple juice, applesauce, apple cider vinegar, and candy apples. Be sure to include several varieties of apples as well. Tape index cards with sentences to each object:

  Apple juice is made from apples.
  Applesauce is made from apples.
  Candy apples are made from apples.
  Apple cider vinegar is made from apples.

  Begin your study of apple products by commenting aloud, "I wonder what other items they make from apples?" Allow the children to independently observe. Then ask them open-ended questions to encourage meaningfully discussion:

  What do you notice by playing here today?
  What is your favorite part about this center?
  What have you learned about apples?

- Make applesauce from the apples that the children brought to school. (Be sure to set aside three of the apple varieties, such as Granny Smith, Golden Delicious, and Empire, for a Math lesson later.) Here is a straightforward, easy recipe I use:

  Simple Applesauce Recipe
  15 apples, mixed variety
  2 tsp. lemon juice
  1 Tbs. sugar (optional)
  1 tsp. cinnamon

  1. Wash and peel the apples.
  2. Using an apple slicer/corer, core and slice all the apples.
  3. Hand out small plastic knives and a small paper plate for each child in a small group. Allow the children to cut some apple slices until all the apples are cut into tiny pieces.

Continue step 3 with other small groups until all the children have participated in cutting the apples. This helps them to feel their powerful contribution to the group and to the classroom's recipe.

4. Place all apple pieces in a large Crock-Pot. Pour the lemon juice over the apples then sprinkle with sugar and cinnamon.
5. Cook on high for 4 hours or until done. Remember to stir on the hour, mashing and mixing all the ingredients.
6. Serve the applesauce as your daily snack.

Math

- Include different-sized apple varieties in a basket at your math center. Give the children a scale and allow them to compare the sizes. Model how to balance two smaller apples, and discuss how they can equal or outweigh one large apple. Allow the children to independently observe and freely explore in this area. During center time, ask the children questions like these:

  What do you notice?
  Which apple weighs most?
  Which apple weighs least?
  What happens if you put more than one apple at one end?

- Create an apple math graph. Using three varieties of apples, such as Granny Smith, Golden Delicious, and Empire, cut each apple into tiny pieces and have the entire group sample only one variety at a time. After trying all three varieties, ask the children which apple is their favorite. On a chart paper, "My Favorite Kind of Apple," make three columns. In column one, draw a green apple and write "Granny Smith"; in column two, draw a yellow apple and write "Golden Delicious"; and in column three, draw a red apple and write "Empire." Next, ask each child to say which apple was his favorite. Have each child write his name in the column representing his favorite sample.

- You can also use the Favorite Apple graph to ask higher-level critical math questions. For instance, ask how many children liked Golden Delicious more than Empire apples? Children will use their higher math abilities for interpreting the graph. Discuss such terms as *most, least,* and *more than.*

- Post your Favorite Apple graph in the classroom. While they are eating applesauce or trying other apple foods, you can remind the children that the applesauce included all three apple varieties.

Blocks and Building

- Continue with the tree house construction from your Fall Leaves theme's Blocks and Building activity. The children will enjoy returning to this favorite center. Discuss all the wonderful things that trees provide us: beautiful color, leaves, and juicy, delicious apples in the autumn season. They also give us a place to put a special tree house. Again, find wonderful tree house design pictures on free Internet sites, print them, and hang them for viewing in your blocks center. Your little construction crew will enjoy time and again developing their own tree house designs.

Using our Favorite Apple graph, I ask Christine how many more children liked the yellow apples more than they liked the green apples.

Language Arts

- Print photos from your Exploring Outside field trip and create a classroom big book. Begin by gluing each of the photographs to a sheet of 11 x 18 inch construction paper. Next, place the photo sheets together in a three-ring binder. Show the children the booklet as you reflect on your field trip or other approach to observing apples.

- Teach the children about writing picture captions. Explain that by adding captions, pictures become livelier and more interesting to readers. Captions can reveal certain information that a picture alone cannot, such as the specific place it was taken or who is in the picture. During group time, write the captions for the pictures of your apple field trip book together. Later include the book in the reading center for all to enjoy.

Reading

- Provide apple books in your reading center for children to explore. Books on other fruit trees provide an interesting connection too. Providing children with various nonfiction books that show how an apple grows and all the things we can do with apples will be beneficial. Fiction books should be provided as well. This is also the perfect opportunity to introduce the legendary Johnny Appleseed story. Some books you can feature include *The Apple Pie Tree* by Zoe Hall and *Apples* by Gail Gibbons.

- Include the language arts activity's apple field trip book in the reading center for children to revisit when they wish.

Writing

- Include sentences that end with the word *apples* on sentence strips. Highlight the word *apples* in a different color for word recognition and one-to-one word reading correspondence. Including pictures for emergent reading skills is an added bonus. Allow the children to write and dictate sentence strips at this literacy station. They will enjoy their illustrations and make a connection to the science and discovery activity as well. Example strips should include these:

  Apple juice is made from apples.
  Applesauce is made from apples.
  Candy apples are made from apples.
  Apple cider vinegar is made from apples.
  Apple cider is made from apples.
  Apple pie is made from apples.

Dramatic Play

- Set up your Autumn Apple's dramatic play center just as you did for Fall Leaves. You can add an autumn apple pie focus by giving the area more of an apple theme. Let the children become pastry chefs while pretending to bake apple pies. Include red play-dough and a basket of wooden toy rolling pins, plastic knives, craft sticks, and apple cookie cutters. Bring in aprons, pot holders, and recyclable aluminum pie plates too. If you have play food, such as artificial fruit and imitation pie slices, include it. The children will enjoy rolling out the dough and creating a pie for you to sample. Tell them they are superb pastry chefs.

Art

- Make fingerpainted apple-shaped *A*s. Start with large fingerpaint paper. Cut each page into a large apple shape. (Hint: Save time by cutting four or five at a time.) Drop a dollop of red fingerpaint on each paper shape, and watch the children have fun spreading red color over the apple shapes. When an entire paper is covered in apple red, have each child finish her project by making an *A* on the paper. Close your lesson by asking the children what sound(s) the letter *A* makes. When they enunciate the short vowel *a,* as in *apple,* praise them by declaring, "Aaabsolutely aaamazing!" I have noticed children's comprehension strengthens when I reinforce their learning with my enthusiasm. A bit of exaggeration with amplified letter sounds goes a long way.

Brittney creates an *A* on her apple paper.

Music

- If you get on virtually any educational website for teachers of young children, you will undoubtedly come across many apple fingerplays and an abundance of apple songs, all sung to one of many classics, such as "Twinkle, Twinkle, Little Star" or "I'm a Little Teapot." Here are lyrics I wrote to be sung to some children's classics. Use singing as a transitional activity, such as after cleaning up at your apple centers or before beginning an apple chart or apple book. Both songs provide a little scientific information.

   Sing "The Apple Started as a Seed" to the tune of "Row, Row, Row Your Boat":

   The Apple Started as a Seed
   The apple started as a seed.
   Now it's big and round.
   It grew and grew and grew and grew,
   Then fell to the ground.

   When finished with the song, pretend to take a bite of an apple, chew, rub your belly, and say, "Yum, yum!"

Sing "I See an Apple in the Tree" to the tune of "Twinkle, Twinkle, Little Star":

I See an Apple in the Tree
I see an apple in the tree.
It started as a little seed.
It started out so very small.
It became a tree after all.
Now it's red, big, and round.
When will the apple fall to the ground?

After singing this song, use the last line as an opportunity to trigger further discussion. Ask the children, "Why do we want the apple to fall to the ground?" and "What happens to the apple once it falls to the ground?" and "When do you think the apple will fall to the ground?"

Closing the Autumn's Apples Theme

Throughout your work with the Autumn's Apples activities, ask children questions that further enhance their comprehension. In your group times, be sure to discuss all the products made from apples. Here are some additional questions you can use during activities and to bring this theme to a close:

What do apples give us?
What have you learned about apples?
What do you like best about apples?

Autumn Theme 4: Perfect Pumpkins

Exploring Outside

If you are lucky enough to have a pumpkin farm or local gardens within walking distance, take the children on a walk outdoors to observe pumpkins. If not, connect with a local pumpkin farm and take your children on a Perfect Pumpkins field trip.

Field trips are a superb way of getting children engaged in their learning experiences. Children truly awaken once they are out in the real world of nature. If field trips are not available in your school budget, walk to a farmers' market where apples, pumpkins, and other produce are sold. A grocery store will do the trick as well. Children always treasure the experience of hands-on instruction. Be sure to take pictures to use later in Perfect Pumpkin integration activities in the classroom.

Throughout your tour, once again ask open-ended questions to help children tune into the fruit farm and all its offerings more closely:

What do you notice?
What do people do with pumpkins?
How long do you think it takes a pumpkin to grow this large?
How do pumpkins get to the store?
What else do you notice?

Teacher Reminder:
You could connect these two autumn activities, Autumn's Apples (page 33) and Perfect Pumpkins, and take your class to an apple- and pumpkin-picking farm.

Role Play Outside

While outdoors, tell the children they get to be pumpkins. Ask them to use "I" statements to share two important things about themselves—for example, "I am an orange pumpkin in the pumpkin patch" and "See how big I am!" Asking children to be specific and identify two important things helps them focus on key elements. It also strengthens their language and comprehension. Have them talk about their pumpkin selves by asking, "Tell me about yourself!" This generates creative thoughts and original dialogue.

Ask other plant-related questions:

How long did it take you to grow?
What do you look like?
How long have you been here?
What do you like about yourself?
What are you waiting for?

Keep the open-ended questions going for more advanced thought and communication development.

Involving Families: Studying Pumpkins at Home

Supply the children with some fun activities to do at home. Mention the activities in your weekly newsletter to families. Explain to families that the optional activities are provided for extra quality time together in nature and involvement in their children's education. Explain that the children are learning about pumpkins. Describe the following nature activities for the families to enjoy at home:

- Ask families, if possible, to send to school with their child small items whose names begin with *P* or *p*. Explain that you will create a phonemic activity in your writing center to go along with your Perfect Pumpkin theme. Ask families to include their *P/p* items in a ziplock bag with the child's and the item's name so that sorting items to send back home will be much easier. Tell families that all *P/p* items will be returned home after your Perfect Pumpkin theme is finished. Thank them for their contribution to your Writing activity lesson (see page 45–46).

- Next, ask families who will be carving pumpkins with their children to send in a picture of the event. Beforehand, send home a half sheet of paper that reads "We carved a ____ pumpkin." Ask families to fill in the blank in this sentence, using words such as *scary* or *funny*, and send it to school along with their picture. During your circle time activities, discuss all the descriptive words that families provided. Thank families in advance for helping their children learn about descriptive words, called *adjectives*.

Integrating Nature: Studying Pumpkins in the Classroom

Bring three or four different sizes of pumpkins from your Exploring Outside field trip to the classroom for further investigation. If possible, also bring squash and gourds and other pumpkin items, such as canned pumpkin for pie making, roasted pumpkin snack seeds, and pumpkins or squash custard or soup. Any or all of these items are perfect for inclusion in the wide range of activities that follow.

Science and Discovery

- Include posters of pumpkin patches in your discovery center. Be sure to include a colorful life cycle picture of a pumpkin as well. Along with your bright posters, put a place card that reads, "Items made from pumpkins." Next, include pumpkin items that do not have to be immediately refrigerated, such as a whole pumpkin itself, canned pumpkin for making pies, roasted pumpkin seeds, and pumpkin extract or pumpkin seed oil. Tape index cards to identify the items, using sentences like these:

  Canned pumpkin comes from a pumpkin.
  Roasted pumpkin seeds come from a pumpkin.
  Pumpkin pie comes from a pumpkin.

  Allow the children to independently observe here. Begin your science and discovery thoughts by asking aloud, "I wonder what other items they make from pumpkins?" During center time, ask the children questions like these:

  What do you notice?
  What is your favorite part about playing here?
  What have you learned about pumpkins?

- Dissect two pumpkins as a group activity. Before beginning, place the pumpkin on a table covered with newspapers. Ask the class what they think they will find inside the pumpkin. After the children have had a chance to respond, discuss the terms *pumpkin pulp* and *pumpkin seeds*. Once the pumpkin top has been removed, allow the children to delve into the pumpkin, pulling out the pulp and seeds with their hands. After the entire pumpkin is empty, rinse it and have the children separate pulp from seed. Dry the seeds on a tray. One tray will be used for eating, the other for a writing activity. The seeds will be ready the following day for roasting, eating, and writing.

- Make roasted pumpkin seeds using one of the following methods.
    1. Brush a cookie sheet with canola oil and spread the pumpkin seeds out on it. Drizzle a bit more oil over the seeds. Salt and roast in a 400 degree Fahrenheit oven for 10 to 15 minutes or until lightly brown.
    2. Heat a tablespoon of canola oil in an electric frying pan. Once heated, add pumpkin seeds and cook until lightly brown. Salt and serve.

Math

- Include a ball of yarn and scissors at this center for measuring the circumference of a pumpkin. Help each child extend the yarn around the pumpkin, encircling its circumference. Cut the yarn and hold it up, saying, "This is how big the pumpkin measures all the way around; this is its circumference."
- Measure the pumpkin with a yardstick or tape measure, and tell the children its size as you write it on a scrap piece of paper.
- On the computer, create a sheet with the sentence "My pumpkin measures this long:_____." Leave space underneath for the children to glue their piece of yarn to the paper. Record its measurement.
- Allow the children to freely explore circumferences in this area using other gourds, pumpkins, and squashes. During center time, while the children measure, ask them questions like these:

    What do you notice?
    Which is the largest?
    Which has the smallest circumference?

Blocks and Building

- Connect your upcoming pumpkin art shape activity with this block activity. Focus on creating shape structures using blocks. As they create their shape structures—for example, a triangle or a square—connect them to the shapes they designed in the art activity above. For instance, say, "Wow, that looks just like the triangle you used for the pumpkin face, only this time it is larger." By providing comparisons, you add more critical thinking.

Language Arts

- Print out photos from your field trip and create a classroom big book. Begin by gluing each photograph to a sheet of 11 x 18 inch construction paper. Next, collect the photo sheets in a three-ring binder. Show the children the booklet as you reflect on your field trip and/or your choice of how you decided to observe pumpkins.

- Teach the children about writing picture captions. Explain that by adding captions, pictures become alive and more interesting to the reader. Tell them that captions can reveal information that a picture alone cannot, such as the location or who is in the picture. Write the picture captions together during a group time. Later include the book in the reading center for all to enjoy.

- Make a web of descriptive sense words describing the pumpkin pulp. In the center of the diagram, write the word *pumpkin*. Add five lines radiating from *pumpkin*, and write *feels, smells, looks, sounds,* and *tastes.* Encourage the children to describe how it felt, smelled, looked, sounded. Write the children's descriptive words underneath the appropriate category. Later add *taste* to the web. After the children have tasted their pumpkin seeds, finish the web by asking them to describe what the seeds tasted like.

Reading

- Provide pumpkin books in your reading center for children to explore. Books on other squashes and gourds will provide interesting connections too. Make available nonfiction that shows how a pumpkin grows. Providing them with books that show all the things we get from pumpkins will be beneficial too. Fiction books should be provided as well. Since the autumn season is well on its way, include jack-o-lantern books for added fun, especially as the Halloween holiday approaches. Some books you can feature include *Pumpkin Pumpkin* by Jeanne Titherington and *The Little Old Lady Who Was Not Afraid of Anything* by Linda Williams.

Writing

- From the Involving Families section, continue with your phonemic lesson with the letter *P/p* at your writing center. Use the *P/p* items the children brought from home. Place them on a tray labeled, "Look at all of our *P/p* items!" Next, on a sentence strip, leave a space to place a *P/p* item from the tray; then write the following: "＿＿ begins with *P/p*." Children will be able to take items from the tray, such as a pencil, pen, paper, purple pony tail elastic, and place it on the blank line and read the sentence independently. Allow older children to write the sentence on paper phonetically. Send home all the children's *P/p* items once you are finished with your Perfect Pumpkin nature theme.

- From your pumpkin dissecting activity, prepare a phonemic lesson with the letter *P/p*. On the computer, create a sheet with the sentence "Pumpkin begins with the letter *P/p*." Leave a blank line beneath it for the children to write the remainder of the sentence "Pumpkin begins with the letter ＿＿." Leave a space for the children to create a *P/p* with pumpkin seeds. This can be left at the writing center for fine-motor and phonemic practice again and again. Or you can copy the paper and allow each child to glue his or her pumpkin seeds to make a letter *P/p*.

Dramatic Play

- Use your Fall Leaves dramatic play center idea here too (page 23). Put the focus on pumpkin pie creations. Let the children become pastry chefs while pretending to bake pumpkin pies. In your dramatic play area, include orange playdough and a basket of wooden toy rolling pins, plastic knives, craft sticks, and cookie cutters. Bring in aprons, pot holders, and recyclable aluminum pie plates for your dramatic play area too. As an added plus, introduce play food, such as artificial fruit and imitation pie slices. The children will enjoy rolling out the dough and creating a pie for you to sample. Once again, remind them they are superb pastry chefs.

Art

- Make a pumpkin face using shapes. Here is what you will need:

  A large circle copied onto orange construction paper, one
    for each child
  Small rectangles cut from green construction paper
  Various small shapes cut from black construction paper
  Glue sticks

Instruct the children to cut their circle from the orange construction paper and to glue the green rectangle stem to it. Allow the children to independently choose which black shapes they want to use for the eyes, nose, and mouth. Afterward, discuss all the shapes they used for creating their pumpkin face.

Music

- On virtually any educational website for early education teachers, you will come across lots of autumn pumpkin fingerplays and a wealth of pumpkin songs, all sung to one of the many classics such as "Twinkle, Twinkle, Little Star" or "I'm a Little Teapot." Try writing your own pumpkin song using one of the many classics. Here is a song you can sing to a children's classic tune. Use it as a transitional activity, such as after cleaning up your pumpkin centers or before beginning a pumpkin book. Sing "The Pumpkin Started as a Seed" to the tune of "Row, Row, Row Your Boat":

> **The Pumpkin Started as a Seed**
> The pumpkin started as a seed,
> Now it's big and round,
> The vine grew and grew and grew and grew,
> A pumpkin on the ground.

Closing the Perfect Pumpkins Theme

Throughout your work with the Perfect Pumpkins activities, ask children questions that further enhance their comprehension. During your group times, be sure to discuss all the wonderful treats we get from pumpkins. Here are some additional questions you can use to bring this theme to a close:

> What do pumpkins give us?
> What have you learned about pumpkins?
> What do you like best about pumpkins?

Autumn Theme 5:
Spider Species

Exploring Outside

Autumn is the perfect time of year to study spiders with your class. Children are fascinated by little lively creatures like spiders. When you add four pairs of legs and four sets of eyes around the Halloween holiday, children's interest perks up even more.

Before observing spiders, have a group time discussion about the nature of spiders. Although there may be many brave little ones in your classroom who would let a spider crawl on their hands and arms, explain that it is best not to allow spiders to do this. When provoked, some spiders do bite, and unless you are a scientist who studies spiders and you thoroughly know all your spiders, you should never allow spiders to crawl on your body.

Explain to the children that they are going to become arachnologists, or spider experts, this autumn. Discuss the terms *arachnid*, *arachnologists*, and *arachnology*. *Arachnids* are a class of joint-legged invertebrate animals that includes spiders and other species. *Arachnology* is the study of these species, and *arachnologists* are the scientists who study spiders, scorpions, and other arachnids. Take your magnifying glasses and scientific minds outdoors for a spider adventure. Bring along some black paper in hopes of finding the perfect spiral orb web to bring back to the classroom.

Once a spider or web is found, ask questions like these:

What is it doing in its web?
Where does it sleep?
What kind of dinner do you think it will eat?

If you find a web without a spider, ask questions like these:

Where do you think the spider went?
What do you notice?
What do you think about the web?
What do you think about the spider?
What else do you notice?

As children respond to discovering the fascination of nature questions, their answers may elicit other discussion and questions for you.

Role Play Outside

While outdoors, tell the children they get to be spiders. Ask children to use "I" statements and to share two important things about themselves, for example, "I am a spider and I have eight legs" and "I can crawl fast; watch me!" Use the statement "Tell me about yourself!" As always, this initiates imaginative thinking and creative talk. By asking them to be specific and to identify two important things about themselves, you will help the children apply essential points to their language and thinking and develop an understanding of the attributes of spiders.

Keep the discussion going by having the children describe themselves as spiders. Ask open-ended questions like these:

Where do you live?
What do you eat/drink?
How do you eat/drink?
Why did you make a web?
What do you do with the insects that land in your web?
What do you look like?
How long have you been here?
What do you like about yourself?
Do you have a family?

Involving Families: Studying Spiders at Home

Supply the children with some fun activities to do at home. Mention the activities in your weekly newsletter to families. Explain to families that the optional activities are provided for extra quality time together in nature and for involvement in their children's education. Explain that the children are learning about spiders. Describe the following nature activities for the families to enjoy at home:

- Ask families to take a walk together outdoors in nature, looking specifically for spiders. Ask the family to come up with one word to describe the particular spider they found. When you send home the newsletter, also provide a half sheet of paper the family can use to write its descriptive word. Tell the families that the descriptive words will be added to your Spider Web of Words chart (see language arts activity, pages 51–52). Thank them for their contribution to your academic lesson.

- Ask families to carefully catch any spider they find in their home in a tissue or cup and show their children how to release it outdoors. Often children will be scared of spiders and stomp on them. Ask families to please teach their children how to respect all of nature, even if these creatures are not their favorites. Reminding children that spiders eat flies and that spiders are helpful for the environment may quell their frightened actions.

Integrating Nature: Studying Spiders in the Classroom

Somewhere in your travels through the school building or grounds, you will come across an orb web. They always seem to form on the outside of my classroom window, so I recommend checking your windows first. Bring a large piece of black construction paper with you to press against the web to capture it, keeping as much of it intact as possible. You will find creative uses for this web in many of the following science and discovery, math, blocks, language arts, reading, writing, dramatic play, art, and music activities.

Science and Discovery

- Include posters of spiders in your science and discovery area. Be sure to include a colorful poster of the typical spider's life cycle. Display pictures of various types of webs as well. Enhance the children's learning by adding labels and interesting information. For example, a picture of a spider in its orb web can include the caption "The spider waits in its orb web for its prey." A language-rich science and discovery area helps children develop their literacy skills too.

- Exhibit an orb web treasure from your Exploring Outside activity.

- If you have a collection of plastic toy spiders and other creepy crawlies, put some on a tray for the children to inspect closely.

- If you find dead spiders, carefully lay them on top of a tissue or cotton gauze and place them under a petri dish. You can keep the petri dish along with a microscope or magnifying glass nearby for the children to examine these creatures more closely.

Math

- Put some plastic toy spiders and bugs in a bucket and allow the children to sort through the bucket freely.

- Later supply sorting trays and model for the children how to sort the plastic toy insects (those with a head, thorax, abdomen and six legs) from spiders and other arachnid creepy crawlies (those with eight legs and other characteristics). Children will enjoy time and again playing with toy creepy crawlies. The repetition also helps them with their sorting and classifying abilities.

Blocks and Building

- Based on the poem "Little Miss Muffet," allow the children to construct sturdy tuffets. Begin by reading "Miss Muffet":

  > Little Miss Muffet sat on a tuffet,
  > Eating her curds and whey.
  > Along came a spider,
  > Who sat down beside her,
  > And frightened Miss Muffet away!

  Ask the children, "What are *tuffets*?" As their answers come pouring in, you may need to remind them that Little Miss Muffet sat on it. Explain that tuffets are small stools. Hang up a banner that reads, "We are building tuffets!" Be sure to include pictures of stools on the banner. During center time, let the children use blocks to construct sturdy child-sized tuffets or stools.

- Connect the action at this blocks and building area with the "Little Miss Muffet" theme in the dramatic play center.

Language Arts

- Create a classroom Spider Web of Words bulletin board about spiders. Begin by covering a bulletin board with orange construction paper. Put this title at the top: "Spiders are . . ." Next, using a ball of white yarn and pins, create an orb web. Be creative!

- Come together as a group and create a web diagram on chart paper to display descriptive words about spiders. Be sure to include all the descriptive words sent in from the children's

Teacher Reminder: You can repeat this activity when discussing Summer's Insects (page 187), Busy Honeybees (page 215), and Picnic Ants (pages 221–222).

fun activities at home. Children will share that spiders are scary, hairy, ugly, creepy, black, tiny, and so on.

- When the children have finished making a spider in the art activity (page 53), give them white crayons. Let them choose one of the descriptive spider words from the chart and write the chosen word on the spider's abdomen. For younger children, you may need to listen to their responses and write the words yourself. More advanced children can phonetically sound out their descriptive words.

- When all the children have created their spiders and have written their descriptive words, staple all their spiders to the bulletin board. The result is the perfect autumn bulletin board, especially around Halloween.

Reading

- Provide spider books in your reading center for children to explore. Include books on arachnids and arachnology. Provide nonfiction books that show different types of webs. There are many great books that describe how helpful spiders are and all the good things they do for nature. These would be good to include, since spiders have a bad reputation and many children (and adults) do not like them. Fiction stories should be provided as well. Include a few spider books that address the Halloween holiday. Some books you can feature include *Spiders* by Gail Gibbons, *Be Nice to Spiders* by Margaret Bloom Graham, and *The Very Busy Spider* by Eric Carle.

Writing

- From your chart paper in the language arts activity, cut out the descriptive words and place them in a bin. Put the bin of words in the writing center. Include premade 8½ x 11 inch sheets that read, "Spiders are ____." Children will be able to pull from the bin a descriptive word, such as *ugly* or *black,* and write it on the blank line. Below the sentence, they can illustrate their statement. Praise them for their writing and illustrating.

Dramatic Play

- Let the children reenact "Little Miss Muffet." Hang up the rhyme in your dramatic play area:

     Little Miss Muffet sat on a tuffet,
     Eating her curds and whey.
     Along came a spider,
     Who sat down beside her,
     And frightened Miss Muffet away!

  Provide some dress-up clothes for Little Miss Muffet. A few bonnets and dresses should do (especially if you want more than one Little Miss Muffet). Provide a place for Little Miss Muffet to sit on her tuffet—any small stool will do. Consider using some of those the children created in the Blocks and Building activity (page 51). Be sure to include a plastic bowl and spoon so she can eat her curds and whey. Don't forget to include some play spiders. The children will enjoy being Little Miss Muffet; many will also want to be the spider who sat down beside her. They will feel their power as they frighten Little Miss Muffet away.

Art

- Make a descriptive spider. Here is what each child will need:

     Two black circles traced onto black construction paper
     Eight strips of black construction paper (for legs)
     Recycled white hole punches for the eyes
     A white crayon for writing the descriptive word on the spi-
        der's abdomen
     Glue sticks

  Instruct the children to cut their circles from the black construction paper. This helps strengthen their fine-motor skills. Glue the abdomen circle to the head circle. Have the children glue four pairs of eyes on each spider's head. Children will enjoy this fine-motor skill. Next, have them accordion-fold each leg strip and glue it to the back of the spider.

  Ask each child to choose a descriptive word to use for the spider. They can choose from the language arts charting activity. Write the word in white crayon on the spider's abdomen. When all the children have finished their spiders, staple them to the "Spiders are . . ." orb web bulletin board created in the language arts activity (pages 51–52).

Music

- Make up your own nonsensical version of the nursery rhyme classic "Itsy Bitsy Spider." Focus on rhyming words and having fun. Begin by singing the classic song together:

  Itsy Bitsy Spider
  The itsy bitsy spider climbed up the water spout.
  Down came the rain, and washed the spider out.
  Out came the sun, and dried up all the rain.
  And the itsy bitsy spider climbed up the spout again.

  Ask the children what else outside in nature a spider could climb up. Then, as a class, come up with various rhyming words for these other objects and sing the song together. For example, notice how you can replace *water spout* with *great big tree*. And you can replace *out* with *free*.

  The itsy bitsy spider climbed up the great big tree.
  Down came the rain, and washed the spider free.
  Out came the sun, and dried up all the rain.
  And the itsy bitsy spider climbed up the tree again.

  Try replacing *water spout* with *tall, tall swing* and *out* with *fling*.

  The itsy bitsy spider climbed up the tall, tall swing.
  Down came the rain, and washed the spider—fling!
  Out came the sun, and dried up all the rain.
  And the itsy bitsy spider climbed up the swing again.

  Make up your group's own nonsensical versions and have fun practicing rhyming with children.

Closing the Spiders Species Theme

Ask children questions that further their comprehension:

What have you learned about spiders?
How do you feel about spiders?

Be sure to include all of the benefits spiders provide us in your group discussion.

Autumn Theme 6: Searching for Squirrels

Exploring Outside

Take the children to a nearby park or into the school yard on a search for squirrels. Autumn is the perfect time to observe them in their typical squirrelly action. In the later part of fall, squirrels frantically gather acorns and other nuts for winter storage.

Before heading outdoors on your squirrel search, explain to the children that often squirrels become startled and run away when people come too close to them. For that reason, the children can best observe and appreciate squirrels, and most other wildlife, from some distance. With luck, they will be able to see the squirrel's superb natural ability to balance itself across telephone wires and bounce from tree limb to tree limb.

Once you or one of the children has spotted a squirrel, ask the children open-ended questions like these:

What do you notice about the squirrel?
Where are they going?
How did they learn to balance like that?
What else do you notice?

Paying attention to the children's responses will bring to your mind more questions as well.

Role Play Outside

While outdoors, tell the children they get to be squirrels. Ask them to move and balance like these acrobatic rodents. Have them pretend to gather nuts and to move swiftly. While they pretend to be squirrels, ask them to use "I" terms to share what they look like and how big they are, and to explain what their fur coat feels like. Ask open-ended questions to develop and strengthen their higher-level thinking skills:

What else would you like to tell me about yourself?
Where do you live?
Do you have a family?
What is the best thing about being a squirrel?
How did you learn to balance like that?

Involving Families: Studying Squirrels at Home

Supply the children with some fun activities to do at home. Mention the activities in your weekly newsletter to families. Explain to families that the optional activities are provided for extra quality time together in nature and for involvement in their children's education. Explain that the children are learning about those well-known acrobatic rodents, squirrels. Describe the following nature activities for families to enjoy at home:

- Ask families to take an autumn walk together, looking specifically for squirrels. Ask them to take a little time to gather some acorns or other nuts and send them to school in a ziplock bag. These items will be used for a hands-on math lesson. If they spot a squirrel, ask them to take a photo and send it to school to include in the science and discovery center. Be sure to thank families in advance for all their help with their child's education and emphasize that creating a strong home/school connection helps their children's education.

- Tell families that their children will be discovering the amazing balance and agility of squirrels. Ask them to practice the art of balance together. Perhaps they could walk on a sidewalk crack or chalk line, practice balancing on one leg or standing on their heads—the choices are endless. Invite the families to send in a photo of their balance activity. Explain that you will place all the pictures in your math center to help the children learn about dexterity.

Integrating Nature: Studying Squirrels in the Classroom

It is not acceptable to bring a wild animal like a squirrel into the classroom, but you can bring back some acorns, other nuts, seeds, bark, twigs, wheat, leaves, and pinecones with you from the

Exploring Outside activity. Having these natural items on hand will help you integrate the idea of squirrels, what they eat, and where they live into your science and discovery, math, blocks, language arts, reading, writing, dramatic play, art, and music activities.

Science and Discovery

- Place pictures of squirrels in your discovery area. The pictures that families sent in can also be included at your science and discovery center. You can look on free Internet sites to find many photos of squirrels and information on their general behavior.

- Along with the color pictures, include the natural items gathered from the Exploring Outside activity: acorns, other nuts (such as beechnuts, chestnuts, and black walnuts), seeds, bark, twigs, wheat, leaves and pinecones.

- Put out two trays for the children to sort and classify the natural items. On one tray, tape an index card that reads, "These items are nuts. Squirrels eat these." On the other tray, tape an index card that reads, "These items are not nuts. Squirrels eat these too." Put the other items squirrels tend to eat on this tray.

- Provide magnifying glasses for a closer look at all the items. Children can freely explore in this area during your center time.

Math

- Include nuts from the Exploring Outside activity. You can also include the nuts that families sent in from their autumn walks. Include ten small paper plates with the number ten written on each one. Place all the paper plates on a large posterboard with the number one hundred on it. The children will be able to group together acorns or other nuts in sets of ten, ten times. Later practice counting by tens up to one hundred together.

Blocks and Building

- Have the children pretend to be ground squirrels and make burrows using blocks, snap-block cubes, and other construction items. Include a bowl of acorns and ask the children to construct planks, inclines, and other slopes for rolling their acorns into the burrow. Whether the acorns make it into the burrow or not, the children will have fun trying.

Language Arts

- Create a chart with facts about squirrels. Include what they eat. Describe types of squirrels, such as the gray squirrel, tree squirrel, red squirrel, ground squirrel, and fox squirrel. Discuss what squirrels look like, including their bushy tails and sharp teeth, and mention their expert balancing abilities.

- Put eight or ten sentences from your chart paper on sentence strips. Use simple factual sentences, such as these:

  > A squirrel eats acorns.
  > A squirrel eats twigs.
  > Some squirrels eat wheat.
  > Some squirrels are gray.
  > Some squirrels are red.
  > Some squirrels have bushy tails.
  > Most squirrels have very sharp teeth.
  > Squirrels can balance very well on tree limbs.
  > Squirrels store food for winter.

  Invite each child to illustrate a sentence.

- Create a classroom nonfiction book. Begin by reminding the children of the differences between fiction and nonfiction. Give simple information and samples of each genre. Create a *Squirrel Facts* title page. Then collect the squirrel-fact sentence strips and the children's illustrations to put into book form. Include a sentence strip, such as "Squirrels eat acorns," followed by the children's pictures of squirrels eating acorns. Next, include another sentence strip fact, such as "Some squirrels are gray," followed by all the illustrations of gray squirrels. Continue in this way until all illustrations are included. Bind the book with three rings or yarn and read it with the entire class. Include it in your reading center for further enjoyment.

Reading

- Provide books about squirrels and other rodents for children to explore. Books about chipmunks and other rodents offer a bonus. Ask your librarian for help in finding some fiction books about squirrels and rodents. Some books you can feature include *Scaredy Squirrel* by Melanie Watt and *The Tale of Squirrel Nutkin* by Beatrix Potter.

- Include the children's *Squirrel Facts* nonfiction book from the language arts activity in the reading center for children to revisit whenever they wish.
- If no one is allergic to peanuts, include them as a snack in your reading area. The children will enjoy acting a little squirrelly while reading the squirrel books.

Writing

- Create predictable sentence strips for all the things squirrels eat. Predictable sentence structures in the writing center will help children feel successful as they learn to read. Allow them to dictate and write from the sentence strips. Place a real nut or a picture of one at the end of each sentence as you display it for the children. By including pictures with your sentence strips, you can help children to work more independently, thus feeling like confident writers. Be sure to include colored pencils, thin-line markers, and blank paper for your creative writers. For your more advanced learners, provide paper with a space for illustration and a few writing lines so they can practice letter formation. Sentences can include these:

> Squirrels eat nuts.
> Squirrels eat seeds.
> Squirrels eat bark.
> Squirrels eat twigs.
> Squirrels eat leaves.
> Squirrels eat pinecones.

Notice that these sentence strips correspond to the items in the science center. Point out to the children the relationships between these sentences and the actual items in the science center to increase their comprehension and integration of the two activities.

Dramatic Play

- Have the children squirrel away food this autumn as winter approaches. Create a stocking-up-before-winter-comes inventory for your dramatic play area. Include labeled play food, such as apples, cereal, and milk, in your play cupboards and refrigerator. Include paper lists that show all the items with check boxes next to each food name. While the children are engaged in the dramatic play area, they can match the food in the cupboard with its name on the list and then check it off. This is a great activity for practicing classification and word-to-word recognition skills. Be sure to copy a lot of these generic lists, because the children will love to check off the inventory again and again.

Art

- Let the children make Nutty Squirrel Sculptures. Make peanut butter playdough and sculpt squirrels (head, body, bushy tail).

  Peanut Butter Playdough
  2 cups of creamy peanut butter
  2 cups of nonfat dry powdered milk
  1 tsp. honey

  Mix the ingredients, adding more powdered milk if the playdough is too sticky. Allow children to create their own unique, nutty squirrel sculptures. After admiring their work, the children can eat and savor the sculptures.

Music

- Sing "The Squirrels Are Storing Nuts" to the tune of "The Farmer in the Dell":

  The Squirrels Are Storing Nuts
  The squirrels are storing nuts.
  The squirrels are storing nuts.
  Autumn is here; winter is next.
  The squirrels are storing nuts.

Closing the Searching for Squirrels Theme

Throughout your work in the Searching for Squirrels activities, ask children questions that further enhance their comprehension. During your group times, be sure to discuss why trees are important. Here are some additional questions you can use during activities and to bring this theme to a close:

What have you learned about squirrels?
What do you find most interesting about squirrels?
What was your favorite activity with squirrels in the classroom, and why?

Autumn Theme 7: Flying Feathers

Exploring Outside

Take children on a nature hike to look for feathers. Autumn is the perfect time for finding them, because fall migration is certain to leave a few feathers in your neighborhood. Whether you live in the North or the South, the East or the West, birds are either leaving or entering your area this beautiful time of year.

Before heading outdoors, show the children a few sample feathers. If you do not have any feathers on hand, ask your science teacher or e-mail colleagues—someone is sure to have some bird feathers. People love to donate—especially if by doing so their cupboards become more organized. You can also purchase synthetic and real feathers from craft stores and education catalogs.

Discuss how people use feathers to make pillows and mattresses, decorate fishing lures, and make quill pens. During your walk, use wonder statements and ask open-ended questions to help strengthen children's thought processes:

Where do you think we might find feathers?
I wonder what kind of bird this feather came from.
I wonder why the bird lost this feather.
What do you notice about the feathers?
What else do you notice?

If you see not only feathers but birds on your nature hike, use more wonder statements, such as "I wonder why birds have feathers" and "I wonder where they are flying to."

Role Play Outside

While outdoors, tell the children they get to be feathers. Ask them, "What do you look like?" and "As a feather, how do you feel?" Encourage them to use "I" statements, such as "I am soft and pointy" and "I help birds fly!" while they are pretending to be feathers. Ask open-ended questions to develop the children's higher-level thinking skills, such as these:

How did you get here?
What do you like about yourself?

Children can also role-play birds, such as turkeys, pheasants, mourning doves, or robins. Once again, use open-ended questions:

What kind of bird are you?
What do you look like?
What do you sound like?
Where are you flying to?
Tell me about your feathers.

Involving Families: Studying Feathers at Home

Supply the children with some fun activities to do at home. Mention the activities in your weekly newsletter to families. Explain to families that the optional activities are provided for extra quality time together in nature and for involvement in their children's education. Explain that the children are learning about feathers and birds, and since turkeys are the number one bird featured in America in November, the study unit ties in nicely with the approaching Thanksgiving holiday. Describe the following nature activities for the families to enjoy at home:

- Ask parents to take a nature hike and send in any feathers they find on their outing. Explain that all of the special feathers that come to school will be displayed in the science area and will be used for making quill writing instruments and an Ojibwe dream catcher.

- Encourage families to take a camera on their hike and take photos of any feathers or feathery creatures they see. During group time, have the children discuss their photographs with the class.

Integrating Nature: Studying Feathers in the Classroom

Bring back to the classroom as many feathers as you find on your Exploring Outside nature hike. Ask families to send in any feathers they find on their autumn walks. You'll use the feathers in the following fun feathery activities related to this theme.

Science and Discovery

- Place a wide variety of feathers in your science and discovery center for children to explore. Placing them in a shallow tub or pan allows children to get their hands on the textures of all of the feathers.

- Provide magnifying glasses and a microscope for more scientific discovery.

- Include posters or colored pictures from free sites on the Internet that show feathers and birds. Be sure to include colorful pictures of peacock, turkey, and other feathers.

Math

- Include a wide variety of feathers for sorting, classifying, counting, and graphing. Provide a posterboard with lines on it to form two columns. Children can sort or chart feathers using the two-column graphing technique, such as small and large feathers, brightly colored feathers and earth-toned feathers, fluffy feathers and pointy feathers, and so on.

Blocks and Building

- Have the children use blocks to build towers. Compare how quickly certain items fall from the top of the towers. Children can use feathers to begin their discovery. Items that fall well include paper clips, glue sticks, cotton balls, coins, and paper.

Language Arts

- Create a "Feathers of Gratitude" door for the month of November. This month is the perfect time for bringing gratitude into the classroom. Involve the children in crafting a group turkey. Begin by making a feather shape and tracing it onto construction paper in autumnal colors. Write this sentence on each feather shape: "I am thankful for ____." Place a picture of a turkey on your door that reads "Feathers of Gratitude." Each child will cut out a feather shape and write what she or he is thankful for in the blank space, drawing a small picture underneath the sentence. Older children can phonetically write out what they are thankful for. Let younger children dictate their responses. Place all the colorful feathers of gratitude around the turkey hanging on the classroom door. All in all, your room will convey appreciation in its entryway.

Reading

- Provide nonfiction bird and feather books with close-up illustrations and pictures of birds and feathers. Fiction and books of American Indian legends about birds will help children develop appreciation and respect for other cultures as well. Some books you can include are *Fine Feathered Friends: All About Birds* by Tish Rabe and *The Feathers* by Felicia Law.

- Deck out your reading area with Ojibwe dream catchers and books about the legend of dream catchers. See the art activity on page 65 to make dream catchers.

Writing

- Make your own quill pens for the children to use. On the Internet, you will find many easy to moderately difficult instructions for making quill pens. Or you may choose to simply provide the children with a large turkey or oversized synthetic feathers that have sharp or spiky tips.

  Provide paper and tempera paint for use with the quill pens. For older children, if you prefer, you can provide calligraphy ink from an office supply or craft store. The children can dip their pens and write. Place your descriptive word chart about feathers in the writing center, and allow the children to use their quill pens to practice writing these words. Remember, the process is what is important here, not the quality of their penmanship. Using quills can help them develop an appreciation for contemporary writing instruments. The children will enjoy taking their pens home and sharing the newfound word *quill* with their families.

Dramatic Play

- Put together a traditional Thanksgiving celebration in your dramatic play center. Add play food and aprons for cooking, and let the children enjoy pretending.

Art

- Especially around Thanksgiving, I have come across many ideas for making Ojibwe dream catchers. The Internet and any thematic teaching magazine focusing on American Indians will provide you with ideas for creating a dream catcher. I keep it simple and do not try to create a perfect weave or a detailed dream catcher. Children simply love the process, and when it is their own unique piece of art, they feel ownership and pride.

  To make a simple, unique dream catcher, you will need a variety of feathers, some colorful beads, yarn, a small paper plate, and a hole punch. Cut out the center of the paper plate and punch holes around its outside edge. Allow the children to weave the yarn through the holes from one end to the other. Every other weave or so, allow the children to thread on a bead or two. Leave 6 to 8 inches of yarn to weave, and tie a bead and feather to hang at bottom of the dream catcher. Connect the art and reading areas by decorating the reading center with some dream catchers that the children can look at while reading about the legend.

Here is a dream catcher created by one of the children.

Music

- You are bound to come across songs featuring feathers on teacher-oriented websites. I am always amazed at how teachers can take virtually any classic youth tune and change the words to connect the song to the theme at hand.

  Here is a song about feathers to help children learn shapes and count to ten. Sing the song while forming a shape, such as a square, triangle, or circle, with all ten feathers. Use it to get the children's attention, or sing it as you move into center time or a new activity. Sing "One Little, Two Little, Three Little Feathers" to the tune of "One Little, Two Little, Three Little Indians":

One Little, Two Little, Three Little Feathers
One little, two little, three little feathers,
Four little, five little, six little feathers,
Seven little, eight little, nine little feathers,
Ten little feathers forming a square.

As you sing the song, put down each feather to form a square that uses all ten feathers. Then sing the song again, this time forming a triangle, a circle, or another shape.

Closing the Flying Feathers Theme

Throughout your work with the Flying Feathers activities, ask children questions to further enhance their comprehension. During your group times, be sure to discuss why feathers are important. Here are some additional questions you can use during activities and to bring this theme to a close:

What have you learned about feathers?
How do feathers help birds?
How have humans used feathers?

Winter Nature Study
December, January, February

Winter Reading List

Here is a list of the books I recommend for children throughout the winter:

Asch, Frank. *Moonbear's Shadow.*
Barrett, Judi. *Cloudy with a Chance of Meatballs.*
Beletsky, Les. *The Bird Songs Anthology: 200 Birds from North America and Beyond.*
Bulla, Clyde Robert. *What Makes a Shadow?*
Eastman, P. D. *Are You My Mother?*
Ehlert, Lois. *Snowballs.*
Flack, Marjorie. *The Story About Ping.*
Ghigna, Charles. *Animal Tracks: Wild Poems to Read Aloud.*
Keats, Ezra Jack. *The Snowy Day.*
Selsam, Millicent E. *Big Tracks, Little Tracks: Following Animal Prints.*
Serfozo, Mary. *Rain Talk.*
Silverstein, Shel. *The Giving Tree.*
Udry, Janice May. *A Tree Is Nice.*

Cherishing Quiet and Restfulness

Winter is the time of year with the shortest days and lowest average temperatures. It is the transition from autumn to spring. If you live in the northern part of the world, snow and ice are associated with winter; storms, cold, unpredictability, dormancy, hibernation, and frost are just a few of its characteristics. The slightest storm may mean a snow day, a change in lesson plans, a twist and turn to our usual daily life. Once winter is here, teachers are ready for the unpredictability of this time of year. We know the daily winter forecast, and we become a strength for children—a solid foundation, their predictability for the season. Teachers can use winter as a time to investigate and observe life. This is a magical season to discover.

My Winter Reflection

As a working adult, I take the four-second walk from my warm home to my cold car in the blustery February winds and, at times, question why I still live where I do. I look back and wonder how I spent so many hours outdoors in our frigid New York winters. I realize my childhood fascination with winter was because we made it fun. I'm finding that lesson about enjoyment more important in adulthood. It is also the one lesson I continue to learn from teaching little ones.

As a child, I would bundle up and wade into the frigid, snow-blown street to my friend's house. Waddling to the center of our neighborhood, we would find the perfect flurry-blown area for our snow buildings. Other children would come out, and in voices muffled by their scarves, they would say, "That's a cool house! Let's put in windows!" Our clan created tunnels, channeling our way down the street sides. When we finished one snow home, we built another. Eventually, snowball fights began. It was boys versus girls, young against old (no one older than thirteen), or those who lived on the left side of the street against those from the right. It took only one hard snowball hit and a little cry to end the war. Collectively, we knew we could all get in trouble for hurting someone. Quickly and cooperatively, we cared for the wounded. Our adventures also included sledding quests on the steepest hill, whipping by frozen streams on toboggans. Winter holds exhilarating and frosty, fun memories in my mind.

Your Winter Reflection

What does winter bring to your mind? Maybe you remember making snow angels or getting into those dreaded snowball fights. Perhaps you found winter a comfortable season because your summer temperatures quite often went above 100 degrees. You took solace in the low humidity and extra-sunny days. Maybe you lived where you could practice snow skiing or ice skating. What has winter meant to you?

Below is a teacher reflection section for you to use during this quiet season. As you begin each season, use the reflection section as a beginning balancing point for your own appreciation of the season. It is a fine place to take in thoughts of nature and all the healthy activities winter has to offer. Reflection is also a helpful balancing source to use when working with little ones. It can strengthen many dimensions of your self, including emotional, spiritual, and intellectual aspects. This again will be a healthy format you can use with all the seasons.

What reminiscent winter story comes to your mind? Which ones will you share with the children? This is another opportunity for you to bring winter and its quiescent nature to the young minds in front of you. Shared stories provide an appreciation for nature on another level and will encourage the children to get outdoors and create their own memorable wintertime stories!

Here are some lists and questions to ponder as the current season enters your spirit and classroom.

What does winter mean to you?

_____

_____

_____

_____

_____

_____

What has this season meant to you in the past?

_____

_____

_____

_____

_____

When reminiscing, what winter stories come to your mind?

_____

_____

_____

_____

_____

How will you take time to enjoy this particular season?

_____

_____

_____

_____

_____

What are you thankful for this winter season?

_____

_____

_____

_____

_____

How will you set the tone for the season ahead?

_____

_____

_____

_____

_____

Are there any special activities you can include to bring in the season in your own way?

_____

_____

_____

_____

_____

Sing in the Season

Begin the season with a song that says good-bye to the season you have just finished and welcomes in the season ahead. By continuing to do this with all the seasons, you help children strengthen their predictive skills. By the end of the year, the children will say to you, "Let's sing the good-bye–hello song!" Be sure to praise them for their strong memory skills. This gives the children a simple ritual for saying good-bye to the season they have just enjoyed and helping them to appreciate change and welcome the season ahead with all of its surprises. Building that healthy sense of saying good-bye, letting go, and surrendering to what is in front of us is another wonderful skill nature can teach us. Sing "Good-bye, Autumn! Hello, Winter!" to the tune of "Good Night, Ladies":

Good-Bye, Autumn! Hello, Winter!
Good-bye, autumn; good-bye, autumn; good-bye, autumn;
We enjoyed you so!

Hello, winter; hello, winter; hello, winter;
We welcome you right now!

Invite Families to Participate

Encourage the children's families to notice winter and explore its conditions. Send home a brief letter to families to introduce your upcoming nature activities for winter. Remember—you are helping tremendously by including families in your getting-children-outdoors mission and wholesome environment education. Ask families to provide either a winter picture or some other type of winter sign, such as evergreen branches, bare branches, thermometers, or anything else that will bring the winter topic to curious young minds. Here is a sample introductory letter to send home:

Dear Families,

Happy almost winter! In preparing for the upcoming winter season in our classroom, we will be asking for your help in the weeks ahead. The children will soon be delving into these winter topics at school:

- Winter's Snowflakes
- Coniferous Trees
- Bird Exploring
- Large and Little Tracks
- Groundhogs, Shadows, and Burrows
- Who Are the Hibernators?
- What's the Weather?

Be on the lookout this winter for our simple nature homework activities. These will all be wholesome, fun family activities that will provide enjoyment for the season, such as taking a walk in nature and looking for pinecones, burrows, winter birds, and other winter signs. In the meantime, please send a simple winter treasure with your child to school. These will be added to our Winter Family Treasures box. Items can include such things as a picture of a fun family winter activity or evergreen branches or pinecones you have found during the winter season. We will be discussing these individual items during our group circle time. Our group time discussions will enhance the children's listening, speaking, reading, and writing skills and provide an opportunity to integrate the seasonal theme into all their learning.

Thank you in advance for your winter contributions. More important, thank you for your involvement in your child's education! As a side note, you are probably well aware that today's children need more time outdoors enjoying nature. They need time to appreciate the simple things our environment has to offer. I value having you join me in this important task.

Here's to celebrating the winter season and all of its gifts.

My best to you,
[insert your signature here]

Decorate a shoe box or other box with wintry-looking construction paper and decorations. Be as creative as you wish. Label the box "Winter Family Treasures." When children have brought their treasure items to school, have them put them in the winter treasure chest. Later let each child describe the original items during your group meeting time.

Then in your weekly newsletters, remind families of any specific requests this season, such as sending in a winter picture or going on a forecast walk. In the newsletters, also mention the upcoming optional home activities that are created to help families and their children connect with nature and all its richness.

Winter Theme 1: Winter's Snowflakes

Exploring Outside

On a day when the forecast brings light snow, bundle up the children and go outdoors to observe the falling flakes. Allow the children to bring along pieces of black felt to catch snowflakes on and magnifying glasses to inspect the snowflakes. Or, if you live where the weather is warmer, pick one of your chillier days and head outdoors with some crushed ice for inspection. Regardless of where you live, viewing frozen water crystals outdoors is magical. The children may want to try to catch a snowflake or two on their tongues. They can also lie on their backs and watch the snow fall from a different angle. Using the magnifying glass and black felt sheets, invite the children to investigate the differences and uniqueness of each snowflake.

Ask open-ended questions:

What does the snowflake look like?
What happens after the snowflakes land on your felt sheet?
Why do you think every snowflake is unique?
What else do you notice?

Be spontaneous, and devise your own snowflake open-ended questions.

Role Play Outside

While outdoors, explain to the children they can be snowflakes. Ask them to fall and act like a snowflake. Begin by suggesting, "Show me how you act as a snowflake." Be sure to also ask open-ended questions to help children develop higher-level thinking skills:

Why are you so quiet?
How come every snowflake is different?

What is special about you?

What were you doing in the clouds before you came down here?

Involving Families: Studying Snowflakes at Home

Supply the children with some fun activities to do at home. Mention the activities in your weekly newsletter to families. Explain to families that the optional activities are provided for extra quality time together in nature and for involvement in their children's education. Explain that the children are learning about the winter season and snowflakes, or if appropriate, rain or sleet. Describe the following nature activities for the families to enjoy at home:

- Ask parents to go on a forecast walk with their children. Ask them to look for signs of the winter season, focusing on snowflakes, ice, sleet, rain, or frost.

- Ask parents to discuss the uniqueness of snowflakes and talk about what uniqueness means to us individually as people.

- Ask families to play outside with snow. Remind them to take time to look at the snow falling from the sky.

- If possible, suggest they gather enough snow together to create three snowballs. Put each snowball in its own bowl. Put one snowball in the freezer, one on a window ledge, and another on a countertop. Allow the children to inspect the snowballs on an ongoing basis and discuss their observations.

Integrating Nature: Studying Snowflakes in the Classroom

Unlike leaves or acorns, which you can carry back to your classroom, snowflakes dissipate quickly once in hand. That is probably why we are so enchanted by beautiful falling snow. Snowflakes in this sense are magical. Captivate your young children by integrating snowflakes (or if appropriate, rain or sleet) into the classroom. Bring a bucket of snow to your science and discovery center for use in other activities.

Science and Discovery

- Put fresh snow in a table or large bin and allow a small group of children to explore snow indoors. Provide mittens for their hands and magnifying glasses and spoons for more scientific discovery. For added fun, include sand shovels and beach toys. Ask the children whether they notice any similarities and differences between playing in sand and snow.

- Always encourage children to draw a picture of what they did in the discovery area. As they dictate their captions, write them on their pictures.

- Provide various styles of thermometers for children to discover how thermometers function.

- As the snow melts, give the children beakers and measuring cups. Show them how they can put a sample of the snow in a petri dish and later examine it more closely.

Math

- Ask a large group of children to come up with their top five favorite things to do in the snow, such as sledding, making snowmen, ice-skating, making snow angels, riding snowmobiles, helping to shovel snow, and building a snow fort. As a group, graph all of the children's favorite snow activities. Discuss the math terms *most* and *least*.

- Allow the children to sort through math tubs, using these three concepts: (1) make patterns with winter attributes, such as sleds, snowmen, and snowflakes, using pictures or actual mini-math items; (2) sort white manipulatives from those of other colors; (3) compare objects of small, medium, and large size, connecting the idea to the sizes of snowballs needed for making a snowman. Model for the children how to pattern winter items, sort colors, or compare and measure the sizes of math manipulatives. All three activities contribute to emerging math skills.

Blocks and Building

- Have the children build towers and compare how quickly certain items fall from the top. Use cotton balls to suggest snowflakes to begin your discovery. Other items to use include paper clips, glue sticks, feathers, coins, and paper.

Language Arts

- As a large group, create a chart titled "Snow." Come up with as many snow words as possible, such as *snowman, snowflake, snowmobile, snowplow,* and *snowball.*

- Write a group story using all of the snow words you thought of.

Reading

- Provide wintry nonfiction books that depict the actual season and its attributes. Fiction about play during the coldest season will pique children's interests as well. Some books you can feature include *Snowballs* by Lois Ehlert and *The Snowy Day* by Ezra Jack Keats.

- Include stuffed toy polar bears, penguins, and other polar animals for the children to snuggle while they read about the Arctic and Antarctic.

Writing

- Include pictures of snow and snowflake stencils at your writing center. Encourage children to create compound snow words and write them with white crayons on dark blue and black paper. Provide sentence strips that incorporate compound snow words. As an example, your strips could include these sentences:

  In winter I make a snowman.
  In winter I ride a snowmobile.
  In winter I throw a snowball.
  In winter I wave "Hi" to the snowplow driving by.
  In winter I see snowflakes fall from the sky.
  In winter I wear warmer clothes.
  In winter I see clouds in the sky.
  In winter I play outside.

  Children can look at and copy these strips. Have the word *snow* highlighted in the compound word to promote word recognition and one-to-one word reading correspondence, in which children isolate each word and then read it. This exercise also develops sight word recognition, such as *in, I,* and *a.* Including pictures to assist children with emergent reading skills is a good idea. Allow the children to write and create at this literacy station.

Dramatic Play

- Make your dramatic play center a dressing room for the winter season. Begin by hanging up a banner that reads, "I dress for winter." Below the title, include a numbered list showing the children which items to put on first as they get ready for winter. I always include mittens last and demonstrate how difficult pulling on and zipping things is if I put on my mittens first. All of this helps children with independent dressing skills. Be sure to have pictures next to each item for your emergent readers. Here is how the list reads:

  1. snow pants

  2. coat

  3. hat

  4. boots

  5. scarf

  6. mittens

  If you do not have one already, include a mirror in your dramatic play center. Next, hang up snow pants, coats, hats, large-sized boots, scarves, and mittens. The children will love practicing their independent dressing skills as they get ready for winter play.

Art

- Cut out several sizes of white circles. Let the children use the circles to make a picture on blue construction paper. Title the art activity "See what I can make with 20 white circles." This activity allows children to count twenty items, using one-to-one correspondence. They also get to use their imaginative ideas and to invent one-of-a-kind wintry images.

- For a sparklier snowflake experience, let the children cover their creations in a mixture of Epsom salt and a bit of water. Pour some Epsom salt into a small container and add just enough water to make a soupy mixture. Let the children paint their art creations, which will dry to a frosty finish, giving them that wintry connection and reflection.

Music

- You are bound to come across snowflake songs on teacher-oriented websites. I created these simple lyrics to help children understand that each snowflake is different and to grasp their own uniqueness. Sing "Snowflakes Falling to the Ground" to the tune "Mary Had a Little Lamb":

Snowflakes Falling to the Ground
Snowflakes falling to the ground,
  to the ground, to the ground.
Snowflakes falling to the ground,
Each special and unique.

I am special and unique,
  and unique, and unique,
I am special and unique.
We're special and unique.

Children sing the first verse while fluttering their fingers high in the sky and bringing them to the ground. They can sing the second verse while pointing their thumbs at themselves.

Closing the Winter's Snowflakes Theme

Throughout your work with the Winter's Snowflakes activities, ask children questions to further enhance their comprehension. In your group times, be sure to discuss interesting facts about snowflakes and other winter precipitation. Here are some additional questions you can use during activities and to bring this theme to a close:

What is interesting about snowflakes (or rain or sleet)?
Why do you think snowflakes (or raindrops) are all different?
What else have you learned about winter's snow (or rain or
  sleet)?

Winter Theme 2: Coniferous Trees

Exploring Outside

Before taking the children on a nature hike to look more closely at coniferous (cone-bearing) trees, remind children that coniferous trees grow cones and stay green all year long. Once you're all outdoors, show them the difference between deciduous trees, which lose their leaves in wintertime, and evergreen, cone-bearing coniferous trees. Take pictures of the coniferous trees you observe to use in your Science and Math activities. Allow the children to feel the different needles, such as the pine spikes, Douglas fir, cedar, and spruce needles, and arborvitae branches.

Ask open-ended questions to help children examine coniferous trees' characteristics more closely:

What do you notice about the coniferous trees?
What do the needles feel like?
Can you hear what they sound like in the wind?
What else do you notice?

Use wonder statements to support the student's development of inquisitiveness and reflection:

I wonder what lives in the tree.
I wonder what kind of coniferous tree this is.
I wonder why they can stay green all year.

Children will become natural scientists when they observe a variety of coniferous trees. As always, be prepared for lively questions and motivating observations!

Role Play Outside

While outdoors, explain to the children that they get to be coniferous trees. Ask them to stand strong like coniferous trees. Have them sway with the winter wind. Launch their role play by suggesting "Tell me about yourself" and inviting children to use "I" statements in response when pretending to be coniferous trees. For example, they might say while standing in a tree position, "Look, I grew pinecones on my arm branches." Be sure to once again ask open-ended questions to help develop their higher-level thinking skills:

What do you look like?
How did you get here?
What do you like about yourself?
Why are you so very important?

Involving Families: Studying Trees at Home

Supply the children with some fun activities to do at home. Mention the activities in your weekly newsletter to families. Explain to families that the optional activities are provided for extra quality time together in nature and for involvement in their children's education. Explain that the children are learning this winter about coniferous, or cone-producing, trees. Describe the following nature activities for the families to enjoy at home:

- Ask parents, if possible, to send in a matching set of coniferous branches, approximately one foot long. Tell families that with their help, you will be preparing a sorting, classifying, and matching math game (see pages 82–83).

- Invite families to take a walk in a local park to see if they can find any tree cones to send in. Explain that their cone contributions will be put in your science and discovery and math centers for more fun as the children learn about coniferous trees.

- Ask parents to once again discuss the importance of trees with their children.

Integrating Nature: Studying Coniferous Trees in the Classroom

Clip some coniferous tree branches (three of each kind) and bring them into the classroom for some interactive learning and fun. Don't forget to bring back lots of pinecones from the ground as well. You'll find many ways to incorporate them in the children's science and discovery, math, blocks, language arts, reading, writing, dramatic play, art, and music activities.

Science and Discovery

- Place one branch of each type of coniferous tree branch in your science and discovery center. Include various cones for the children to investigate as well. Include some of the Exploring Outside pictures you took of various coniferous trees and label them—for example, *cedar, Douglas fir, white pine, blue spruce.* You can also print some pictures from free Internet sites. A nonfiction book with factual details about coniferous trees is another helpful item for the center. Provide magnifying glasses for more scientific discovery. During center time, engage in meaningful dialogue with the children by asking open-ended questions:

    What do you find special about playing here today?
    What do you notice at the discovery center?
    What have you discovered?

Math

- Create a sorting, classifying, and matching game for your math center, using branches from the Exploring Outside activity and from those that families sent to school. Provide pictures of local coniferous trees. The photos can be some of those you took exploring outside or ones found on free Internet sites. Label the back of the photos with captions, such as "This is a white pine branch" or "This is a cedar branch." Allow the children to match up branches, sort the different limbs, and classify the stems that correspond to the pictures of coniferous trees.

- For additional math-time enjoyment, include sets of pinecones for sorting, classifying, and matching.

- During math center time, ask meaningful questions of the children:

What do you find special about playing here today?

What do you notice at the math center?

Why did you sort the branches like this?

Blocks and Building

- Discuss how trees provide shelter for birds and other animals. In your shelter discussion, describe the important ways trees provide humans with shelter. Talk about all the things made from trees: homes, wooden furniture, toys, and paper. Encourage the children to use the blocks to make different homes. When the children share their creations with you, praise them while using their newfound vocabulary word, *shelter*. Tell them, "That shelter is awesome! It looks like it would keep a family warm and cozy."

Language Arts

- Create two columns on chart paper, one labeled "Coniferous" and the other "Deciduous." As a large group, discuss all the wonderful things that trees give us. Write the children's responses in one or both of the columns, as appropriate. For instance, under the Deciduous column, be sure to include apples, bananas, other fruits, and colorful leaves. Under Coniferous, you will probably mention green color all year, cones, nuts, and Christmas trees. In both columns, you will want to indicate that trees give us oxygen, shade, protection, paper, wood, and homes for wildlife. Adding simple drawings next to each response will help the children's early reading skills. This activity could also be created as a Venn diagram.

- Print out 8½ x 11 inch sheets of paper that read, "A coniferous tree gives us ____," and other sheets that read, "A deciduous tree gives us ____." Allow the children to choose one fact from the chart and give them the corresponding paper to write and draw on. If the child chooses a fact that is included under both the Deciduous and Coniferous columns, ask him to choose which tree he would like to illustrate. By doing this, you are also able to check for understanding. For younger children, write their response on the blank line, such as "apples." Then allow the children to illustrate their big book pages. Allow more advanced learners to write their own responses from the classroom chart.

- Collect the children's illustrated 8½ x 11 inch sheets and bind them, using three rings or yarn ties. Title the book *All Trees Are Special—A Book about Coniferous and Deciduous Trees*. Read the book to the entire class. Afterward, include it in your reading center for the children to enjoy.

Reading

- Provide nonfiction tree books that depict the differences between coniferous and deciduous trees and their attributes. Fiction that emphasizes the importance of trees will help strengthen children's appreciation of trees too. Some books you can feature include *A Tree Is Nice* by Janice May Udry and *The Giving Tree* by Shel Silverstein.

Writing

- Create a "Trees Are Special" writing area. From the language arts chart, make individual predictable sentence strips that include special tree facts. Include sentences such as these:

  Trees give us shade.
  Trees give us apples.
  Trees give us paper.
  Trees give us wood.
  Trees give us nuts.

  Including pictures on the sentence strips will help develop the children's emergent reading skills. They can practice reading and writing from these strips. To encourage the children in early word recognition, use a green-colored marker to write the word *Trees*. These literacy gestures help children with word recognition and one-to-one reading correspondence, wherein children point to each word to isolate it, and then read it. Allow the children to write and create at this literacy station.

Dramatic Play

- Place an artificial tree in your dramatic play center and allow the children to practice their fine-motor skills by decorating it. Include strips of colored construction paper and glue sticks, and let the children create beautiful tree chains. While everyone decorates the tree, discuss a bit of history regarding the Christmas tree. Keep it simple, and discuss how in olden days people decorated trees with candy and paper ornaments. If you have older children present and want to delve more into the history, this is a great opportunity to do that as well.

Art

- Make an evergreen wintry weather picture. Here is what you will need for each child:

  9 x 12 inch blue construction paper for the sky background
  Various sizes of triangular green cutouts for the evergreen trees
  Various sizes of rectangular brown cutouts for the tree trunks
  Glue sticks
  Watered-down white tempera paint and a toothbrush for splattering winter snowflakes

  Before beginning the art project, review shapes and colors with the children. Allow the children to glue various evergreen tree shapes to the blue background. Tree trunk rectangles can be glued on top or underneath the triangles. To finish the picture, add a little winter weather by dipping the toothbrush into the watered-down white tempera paint. Splatter the paint by using your thumb to pull back on the toothbrush bristles and letting the paint spray onto the coniferous trees and blue sky picture.

Music

- Once again, you are likely to find coniferous tree songs on teacher-oriented websites. We teachers have a way of taking any classic youth tune and changing the words to include whatever we want children to remember. Young children and music go together hand in hand: it is amazing how comprehension takes hold when you set your scientific information to a timeless tune. Here is a song about coniferous trees, "Coniferous Trees Make Cones," which can be sung to the tune of "The Farmer in the Dell":

  Coniferous Trees Make Cones
  Coniferous trees make cones.
  Coniferous trees make cones.
  Coniferous trees stay green all year,
  And coniferous trees make cones.

Closing the Coniferous Trees Theme

Throughout your work with the Coniferous Trees activities, ask children questions to further enhance their comprehension. In your group times, be sure to discuss why trees that stay ever green are important. Here are some additional questions you can use during activities and to bring this theme to a close:

What are coniferous trees?
What are deciduous trees?
What do trees give us?
What do trees give other animals?

Winter Theme 3: Bird Exploring

Exploring Outside

Winter is a fine time to look for birds in your area. Regardless of where you live, some local birds are permanent residents who have adapted to the winter season in your area. If you live in a southern region, you can also observe birds that have migrated.

Before heading outdoors for your bird-watching, teach children the term *ornithology*, which refers to the scientific study of birds. Tell them they are going to be ornithologists, or bird scientists, this winter. Ornithologists first begin by identifying whether the animal they see is actually a bird. Ask your future ornithologists how to tell whether a bird is really a bird. Some of your children may say that birds lay eggs, fly, and have beaks. Once the mention of feathers enters your group discussion, become excited, because that is how all birds are identified. Explain to the children that birds are the only animals that have feathers. (You can remind the children of the feather-finding field trip they took in the fall.)

Take a walk and watch for birds in your area. Bring your camera, and with luck, you will be able to snap some great shots! Look in the trees for nests too. If you are walking in a residential area, keep your eyes open for homes that have bird feeders. Point out the feeders and explain to the children that many birds work very hard in the winter season to find food, and sometimes people help them.

When someone has noticed a winter bird, ask the children open-ended questions to develop language skills:

Do you think that bird migrated here or lives here year-round? Why?
What do you think its feathers do for it?
Where does it get food from?
What else do you notice?

Role Play Outside

While outdoors, explain to the children that they get to be birds. Begin by asking, "How can you fly—will you show me?" or "How was your day today, Bird?" Ask the children to fly and land like birds. This will help the children to get into their bird role. Encourage the children to use "I" when they role play as birds. For example, they can say, "I am a bird flying high in the sky!"

As always, asking open-ended questions will help develop children's higher-level thinking skills. Here are some examples you might use:

What do you do as a bird?
Where do you get your food from?
Where do you live?

Involving Families: Studying Birds at Home

Supply the children with some fun activities to do at home. Mention the activities in your weekly newsletter to families. Explain to families that the optional activities are provided for extra quality time together in nature and for involvement in their children's education. Explain that the children are learning about birds. Describe the following nature activities for the families to enjoy at home:

- Ask families to send in bird feeder donations, such as small bags of popcorn and cranberries, for use in the Math activities, pages 89–90. Tell them you will be doing two separate math lessons and helping feed the birds as well.

- Ask families to send cardboard milk carton donations for making birdhouses for an Art activity, page 92.

- After children have done the related Science, Math, and Art activities, invite families to find a special tree in which to hang their birdhouse and their bird feeder.

Integrating Nature: Studying Birds in the Classroom

Certainly you won't be bringing any birds back to the classroom. However, if you find any nests on the ground after a windy day, bring these back with you. Feel free to take pictures of any birds you see in your Exploring Outside activity. These will be interesting for the children to look at as they reflect on their prior bird knowledge. Include the pictures in your learning centers.

Science and Discovery

- Place pictures of various birds in your science center. These can be from the photos you took on your Exploring Outside activity or from the Internet. Include pictures of nests too. If you are able to supply a real or artificial bird nest or two for this center, that will be a bonus. Bring out some of the feathers from autumn's Flying Feather activities. Allow children to freely explore these objects.

- Encourage children to draw pictures of what they observed in the science and discovery center and dictate their captions to you to write on the illustration paper.

- Winter is the perfect time for decorating trees outside with bird feeders. Help the children make pinecone bird feeders. They begin by spreading peanut butter over a large pinecone. The children love to do this with a craft stick. Sprinkle birdseed onto wax paper. Roll the peanut butter–covered cone on the birdseed until the cone is completely covered in seeds. Tie the top of the cone with yarn and send it home in a small brown lunch bag. Families will be able to find the perfect tree for hanging their bird feeder.

Math

- Ask families to send a donation of goodies to help feed the birds this winter. Tell them they can provide a ziplock bag of popcorn or cranberries. When all the children have brought their donations to school, make a live math graph using all the bags. On a table or other surface, line up all the bags of popcorn in a column, then line up all the cranberry baggies in another column. Discuss the graph terms *most, least,* and *how many more than.*

- When you are finished with the graph, let the children use its contents to make another type of bird feeder. This time, form an A-B pattern bird feeder by stringing popcorn, then cranberries, then popcorn, then cranberries. Put all the bags, strings, and plastic needles in the math center and allow the children to make patterned-string bird feeders to take home to their families to hang in trees near their home.

Blocks and Building

- Allow the children to use blocks of all types to create places for their feathery friends to perch. If you have some artificial birds from a craft store, include them here for a fun perching, balancing act. Otherwise, e-mail your colleagues to ask them to check their closets (or holiday decoration boxes) for artificial plastic birds. I'm always surprised by what my colleagues can find. If no plastic birds appear at your classroom door, print pictures of birds and glue them on folded sheets of paper. Children will have fun creating places for these toys (or pictures of birds) to perch.

Language Arts

- While passing around a few choice bird feathers from your science and discovery center, chart descriptive words the children can use to describe the feathers, such as *soft, smooth, gentle, pretty, black, shiny*, and *beautiful*. Praise the children for using so many descriptive words. Tell them their vocabulary is growing.

- Chart how humans use bird feathers—for example in pillows, blankets or quilts, sleeping bags, and mattresses. Bird feathers are used for filling quilted winter coats too. Colorful feathers from peacocks and pheasants decorate fishing lures and arrows. Before pencils and pens, quill pens were used for writing, like those the children used in the writing center in autumn.

Reading

- Provide bird books for children to explore. Make available nonfiction that depicts birds' attributes. Fiction should be provided as well. Some books you can feature include *The Story about Ping* by Marjorie Flack, *Are You My Mother?* by P. D. Eastman, and *The Bird Songs Anthology: 200 Birds from North America and Beyond* by Les Beletsky.

- Provide feathers for your reading center. Children can use the feathers to point to the words they know, such as *bird, nest*, and *birdhouse*.

Writing

- Allow the children to write and create independently at this literacy station. Teach some facts about birds to your future ornithologists by including facts on sentence strips in the writing center. Be sure to make the strips predictable—that is, ensure that the sentences' structure is the same. (This is a helpful technique to use in developing early skills for your young reader and writers.) Include a different fact about birds on each strip—for example, "All birds have feathers" or "All birds lay eggs." Create many of these strips so the children can view and copy these sentences and draw pictures next to their writing. Highlight the word *bird* in a different color to improve word recognition. Because the sentences are predictable, children will be able to point to each word when they read.

- Children feel successful in their emergent reading abilities when they can name a word by recognizing its image first. Consider including a feather photo or drawing after the words on the sentence strips to help early readers.

- For advanced readers, provide a twist at the end of the strips' predictable sentence structure. By simply changing one word, you will challenge your readers. For example, change the word *all* to *some* in a few bird-fact sentences. Example strips can include these:

  Some birds make nests.
  Some birds eat worms.
  Not all birds can fly.

Teacher Reminder: Birds that don't fly include ostriches, penguins, and emus.

Dramatic Play

- Include bird feeders, bird food, a bird bath, and some binoculars to create a beautiful, imaginary bird sanctuary. If you have artificial birds to place around, great! Otherwise, hang pictures of birds in your dramatic play center. If you are fortunate, you may find a colleague who will agree to bring in her pet bird and cage for a day. Regardless, children can bird-watch, holding up the binoculars and saying, "Shh! Do you see that one over there? Isn't it beautiful?" They only need a little invented fun to develop an amazing respect for these delightful feathery creatures.

Art

- Let children make birdhouses. Here is what you will need:

  Cardboard milk carton from the donations families send to
    school
  Tempera paint
  Yarn or string to hang the birdhouse
  Small wooden dowel or pencil for the bird to perch on

  Begin by cutting a 2-inch hole in the middle of one side of the carton. This will be the birdhouse's entrance. Allow the children to paint their entire carton a solid color. When the paint is dry, they can poke a dowel 2 inches below the house entrance. If they like, they can then paint unique designs on their birdhouses. Punch a hole in the top and thread it with string so families can easily hang their unique birdhouse in a tree of their choosing.

Music

- Here's a song to help children remember what distinguishes birds from other animals—feathers! Sing "Birds Are Special" to the tune of "Bingo":

  Birds Are Special
  Birds are special.
  We know why.
  Feathers help them fly.
  B-i-r-d-s
  B-i-r-d-s
  B-i-r-d-s
  Feathers help birds fly!

Closing the Bird Exploring Theme

Throughout your work with the Bird Exploring activities, ask children questions that will further enhance their comprehension. In your group times, be sure to discuss what makes a bird a bird. Here are some additional questions you can use during activities and to bring this theme to a close:

  How do we know a bird is a bird?
  What have you learned about birds?
  What are some other interesting facts you know about birds?

Winter Theme 4: Large and Little Tracks

Exploring Outside

Children will love the magical wintertime outdoors even more when it involves inspecting mysterious tracks. Their curious minds will naturally want to follow animal footprints as they wonder what interesting creatures made the tracks.

Before you and the children head outdoors to look for tracks, get some books from the library to show the children pictures of interesting animal tracks. Present them with various sizes of tracks, from mice to moose and everything in between. Then put on boots and winter gear for an animal track quest.

When you're outdoors, allow the children to make their own tracks in the mud or snow. Compare all the different boot prints. Then move to where you are likely to find animal tracks. Look around trees and near the edges of school grounds where animals leave tracks.

When someone finds a set of tracks, ask the children open-ended questions, including these:

What type of animal tracks do you think these are?
Why do you think the tracks are here?
How long will the tracks be here?
What would happen if we followed the tracks?
What else do you notice?

Role Play Outside

While outdoors, explain to the children they get to be the animals that left the tracks. Ask them to move like those animals. Perhaps they will want to get down on all fours, leaving their front and back tracks in the snow. Comment, "I notice your tracks—where are you going?" Encourage the children to use "I" statements when they role-play; for example, they may say, "I am leaving tracks." Continue by asking, "What do you look like?" and "Show me how you move and leave tracks in the snow."

Asking open-ended questions helps children to develop their language skills and strengthen their thought processes:

What can you tell me about yourself?
What are two important things I should know about you?
What is the best thing about being you?

Involving Families: Studying Animal Tracks at Home

Supply the children with some fun activities to do at home. Mention the activities in your weekly newsletter to families. Explain to families that the optional activities are provided for extra quality time together in nature and for involvement in their children's education. Explain that the children are learning about animal tracks this winter season. Describe the following nature activities for the families to enjoy at home:

- Ask parents to go on a nature hike with their child, specifically to look for tracks. Have them help their child identify what type of tracks they notice on their short walk. Send home a half sheet of paper with the question, "What kind of animal tracks did you see on your nature hike?" Include a space for families to record what type of tracks they saw, either filling in a blank line or drawing the track on the paper, whichever you've requested. After families have returned their papers, you will use the information for the math charting activity on page 96.
- Invite families to make their own tracks by walking through a puddle, mud, or snow, and then onto pavement. Suggest that they look at the different family members' tracks to see what similarities and differences they notice.

Integrating Nature: Studying Animal Tracks in the Classroom

If you ask young children when they are outside viewing animal tracks what animal they think made those tracks, their excited, number one response will be "Maybe it's a dinosaur!" Second most common is the animated reply, "I think it's a bear." Our theme will set curious young minds to seeking big answers to these footpath mysteries. What follows are activities for keeping the magic of Large and Little Tracks going in your classroom in the areas of science and discovery, math, blocks and building, language arts, reading, writing, dramatic play, art, and music.

Science and Discovery

- Include posters of animal tracks with identification and labels, such as deer tracks and mouse tracks.

- Discuss with the class how tracks can also be fossilized over millions of years. Include some fossils and magnifying glasses in your discovery center too. If you do not personally have any rock fossils in your science cupboard, ask a science teacher or friendly geology buff or e-mail colleagues. Someone is likely to have a few you can borrow.

- Introduce the game Name That Print. Put out playdough at the discovery center and a tray of ten items, which can include such things as a small block, paper clip, pencil, and plastic cup. Children can play this game by taking turns naming that print. The child who is chosen to name that print turns around and closes his eyes. Another child makes a print in the playdough with one of the objects from the tray. Then she announces, "Okay, name that print." The first child opens his eyes and turns around to view the new playdough print. Then he names the object that made that print. After he guesses, the playdough is smoothed out for another round, and the second child hides her eyes and tries to name that print.

Math

- Help children play a kinetic footprint counting game. Trace ten sets of shoe prints onto 8½ x 11 inch paper. On a left shoe print, write the numeral 1 and draw one dot below the number. Finish the left shoe print by writing *one* below the dot. Do the same with the number 2 on a right shoe print. Continue the sequence until you have numbered all ten sets and reached the number 20. Children can sequence the numbers 1 through 20 by walking around the room, placing the footprints in numerical order. The dots are for those children who are still learning numbers and need to use one-to-one correspondence to name the number. More advanced learners can read the numbers at the bottom of each footprint. All the children will enjoy making footprints in the classroom. For even more fun learning, ask them questions, such as "How many footprints is it from the sink to the door?"

• Play a concentration game that will not only help with identifying, classifying, and matching, but reading too. Make up cards of animal track prints to match with the animal that makes those tracks. On each card, draw a picture of a mouse, bird, fox, rabbit, deer, or dog. Cut and glue the pictures to index cards. Make another set of cards with each animal's tracks. Below each track, label what type it is, such as a deer track or bird track. For younger children, you can include small animal pictures at the bottom of these cards to help them play this game independently with peers.

• Create a graph using tally marks. Title your large chart paper "What type of animal tracks did you see on your family nature hike?" On one side of the graph, write the names of the tracks families commonly mentioned seeing, such as deer, cat, dog, fox, raccoon, rabbit, and mouse. At the bottom, write "other." You are sure to receive some atypical responses, such as grizzly bear or dinosaur. As each child provides you with the family's half sheet of paper, read it out and tally the tracks they came across. After tallying the last response, count your tallies. Discuss with children the advantages of using tally marks and counting by fives.

Teacher Reminder:
Similar tracks appear in the Language Arts and Writing activities, integrating the children's learning across these three centers.

Blocks and Building

• Have the children create a large labyrinth using the blocks. They can then walk in and out of the maze, using careful steps to avoid knocking apart or disordering the labyrinth. Young children love to move! By engaging their large-motor skills to the seasonal themes, you are encouraging the children's positive movement within the classroom.

Language Arts

• Make a fun conjecture book, *Who Made That Track?* Not only is this book enjoyable because children get to speculate which animal made the animal track, but it is also predictable, so the children feel proud that they can independently read it. On the computer, create a page that simply reads, "Who made that track?" Print out several copies of the page. Next, copy or make your own animal track on each page. Be sure to include little tracks, such those from a mouse, a bird, or a squirrel. Include medium tracks, such as those for a fox or a rabbit. Then add large tracks, like those of deer, moose, or elk. You can make the track pictures by referring to an animal track book from the library or samples on the Internet. After each page, record which animal made that track—for example, "A mouse made that track." Make sure each sentence is predictable and reads the same way: "A fox made that track" and "A deer made that track." This repetition will help the children develop their early reading skills.

- Allow the children to illustrate the animal they want to represent. Expand the *Who Made That Track?* book to include their illustrations. Put the entire book together, starting with the pictures of the smallest tracks and moving toward the largest ones. This is the order the pages should follow:

> Page 1: Who made that track?
> Page 2: A mouse made that track. *[Include all the children's illustrations of mice tracks.]*
> Page 3: Who made that track?
> Page 4: A bird made that track. *[Include all the children's illustrations of bird tracks.]*
> Page 5: Who made that track?
> Page 6: A rabbit made that track. *[Include all the children's illustrations of rabbit tracks.]*
> And so on.

For the children to claim more ownership and fun, include a boot print on the second-to-last page that reads, "Who made that track?" and end with a page that reads, "I made that track!" As you did with the other track pictures, copy or make a small boot print on this last page. Read the book with the entire class and praise the children for their strong reading abilities.

Reading

- Provide nonfiction books about animals and animal tracks in your reading center for children to explore. Include fiction that discusses making tracks and shapes in mud, snow, sand, and earth. Some books you can feature include *Animal Tracks: Wild Poems to Read Aloud* by Charles Ghigna and *Big Tracks, Little Tracks: Following Animal Prints* by Millicent E. Selsam. Children will enjoy the variety you offer.

Writing

- Allow the children to write and create at this writing center. Use the corresponding writing track activity to strengthen the connection between the language arts activity and writing. Provide sentence strips with simple images of animal tracks. Predictable

Teacher Reminder: All in all, predictable books are classics for your reading center. The children always enjoy the satisfaction of being able to read independently and also treasure viewing one another's artwork. Use the correlating Writing track activity to strengthen the connection with this Language Arts activity.

sentences will help early readers and writers create independently at this center. Example sentence strips can include these:

A mouse makes tracks.
A rabbit makes tracks.
A deer makes tracks.
A dog makes tracks.

After the animal word in each sentence, include a picture of that animal. At the end of each sentence, include a simple drawing of that animal's tracks.

Dramatic Play

• Since tracks are made by feet, add a variety of shoes to your dramatic play center along with a small poster that says, "Walk a Mile in My Shoes!" Offer all types of shoes, including ballet slippers, mountain climbing boots, jogging shoes, and tap shoes. You can even put some walking casts in your center for the children's large-motor skill development. It is amazing how many varieties of shoes you can find at a local thrift store. Often when these stores know you are buying the shoes for use in a classroom, they will give them to you or allow you to borrow them. (Keep in mind precautions recommended in regard to used clothing. Be sure to check your school's "Right to Know" policy, which should include detailed information on use of chemicals, before treating gently used shoes with a safe disinfectant.) Allow the children to try on various shoes and practice walking in them. Ask them questions, such as "How do you feel wearing those shoes?" and "What are your favorite shoes so far, and why?" to elicit extended responses from them and to improve their language expression.

Art

• Here is a twist to the classic garden stone gift that connects it to the "Little to Large Tracks" theme. Have the children create a handprint by placing it in plaster of paris. Or have them make a handprint in concrete for an outdoor stepping-stone. To individualize their handprints, children can add shells, tiny stones, glass beads, or flat colored glass.

Both plaster of paris and cement are a bit goopy, but the small mess is worth the timeless hold of capturing a small handprint for a family gift. Use heavy-duty plastic plates for your mold. Follow the manufacturer's directions on the packaging. Be sure children lather up afterward and wash thoroughly. Let their individual tracks completely dry, which takes a day or so. Remove the handprints carefully. Write in permanent marker on the back, "Tracking ____'s Childhood." Let each child write her own name on the blank line. Date it and wrap it in tissue or newspaper. For added protection, place it in a paper shopping bag before sending it home.

Music

- Here is a song to help children predict whose track is in the ground. If you are indoors, hold up a picture of a track as you sing this song and let the children predict. Sing "Large and Small Tracks" to the tune of "Frère Jacques":

Large and Small Tracks
Large and small tracks,
Large and small tracks,
In the ground,
All around.
I wonder whose track this is! *[Hold up the picture, or point to the track if you are outdoors.]*
I wonder whose track this is! *[Hold up the picture, or point to the track if you are outdoors.]*
Large and small tracks!
Large and small tracks!

Afterward, ask the children to tell you which animal made that track.

Closing the Large and Little Tracks Theme

Throughout your work with the Large and Little Tracks activities, ask children questions to further enhance their comprehension. In your group times, be sure to discuss interesting facts about the animal tracks they've studied. Here are some additional questions you can use during activities and to bring this theme to a close:

What are animal tracks?
How can we tell what kind of animal leaves certain tracks?
What have we learned about animal tracks?

Winter Theme 5: Groundhogs, Shadows, and Burrows

Exploring Outside

If you live in the United States or Canada, you have probably seen at least one of the well-known members of the animal family that includes marmots (also called groundhogs), woodchucks, chipmunks, and squirrels. Needless to say, in the heart of winter, children will enjoy being part of the old legend and tradition of Groundhog Day. To observe groundhogs or woodchucks, your best bet is to review some Internet sites and library books. Children will enjoy viewing all the pictures of the famous groundhog, Punxsutawney Phil. After seeing pictures, some children are bound to realize, "Oh yeah! I've seen one in my backyard."

For your Exploring Outside activity, focus on shadows and burrows. Take a nature hike, noticing all the shadows along your way. Be sure to be on the lookout for burrows too. Once outdoors, bring attention to your own shadow and those of the children. Children can wave to their shadows and to the shadows of their friends. Throughout your walk, point out nature's shadows of such things as trees, bushes, flowers, and birds.

As you see shadows, ask open-ended questions like these:

Why is the shadow so long or so short?
Do we always have shadows?
What if the sun isn't out?
Where do our shadows go when we are inside?
What else do you notice?

Burrows are often found near trees and other sheltered places. Remind the children that a burrow is not only an animal's shelter but also its home. Explain to them that they shouldn't get too close to the burrow so they won't scare any animals that may be living there.

When you find a burrow, ask these and other open-ended questions:

Who do you think lives in there?
What do you think it looks like inside the burrow?
How might it feel to be inside the burrow?
What else do you notice?

Provide such wonder statements as these to prompt the children to imagine:

I wonder if this is the animal's back door or front door.
I wonder what it has inside its home.
I wonder why it made its burrow here.

Role Play Outside

While outdoors, explain to the children that they get to be shadows. Help them get into the role of shadow by first reminding them that shadows are quiet. Invite them to move and act as shadows. After a few moments, wonder aloud, "If shadows could talk, I wonder what they would say." Remind children to use "I" statements to respond as you ask them about themselves as shadows. "Share two important things about yourself!" creates an imaginative conversation.

Use open-ended questions to develop higher-level thinking in the children:

How are you today?
Tell me about yourself.
What do you look like?
How do you feel?
Why are you always dark?
What do you like about yourself?
Where are you going today?

Involving Families: Studying Groundhogs, Burrows, and Shadows at Home

Supply the children with some fun activities to do at home. Mention the activities in your weekly newsletter to families. Explain to families that the optional activities are provided for extra quality time together in nature and to involve them in their children's education. Explain that the children are learning about shadows, groundhogs, and burrows. Describe the following nature activities for the families to enjoy at home:

- Tell families that the children are learning about burrows and the term *shelter*. Communicate that you will be discussing the kinds of shelters people live in. Ask families to describe what type of housing they live in. Their answers will help you in creating a math graph in the classroom (see Math activity, page 103). Send home a half sheet of paper titled "What kind of shelter do you live in?" Include several options with boxes to check, such as apartment, house, trailer, and others.

- Ask families to pick a sunny winter day to go on a shadow nature hike. While on their walk, suggest they point out all the shadows they see and discuss their characteristics. Remind the adults to ask open-ended questions, such as these, to strengthen their children's language skills:

  Why is the shadow so long (or so short)?
  I wonder if our shadows are always with us.
  What if the sun isn't out?
  Where do our shadows go when we are inside?

Integrating Nature: Studying Groundhogs, Burrows, and Shadows in the Classroom

This theme is a surefire hit because of children's natural curiosity and love of mystery and animal life. If you ask children, "What do you think lives in that burrow?" their inquisitive minds begin searching for answers. In addition, the shadow topic naturally seems mysterious, with all the silhouettes and darkness attached to it. Below are ideas for incorporating groundhogs, burrows, and shadows in the areas of science and discovery, math, blocks and building, language arts, reading, writing, dramatic play, art, and music.

Science and Discovery

- Display posters of groundhogs and other large rodents. Include shadow pictures as well. Provide a light projector, flashlights, and a blank posterboard for making shadows. Tape the posterboard to a wall and plug in the light projector nearby. If you do not have an electric outlet nearby, provide a flashlight for your center. When the projector light or flashlight is aimed at the posterboard, the children can stand at varying distances between the light and posterboard to make close-up and far-away shadow images with their hands and fingers. Allow the children to observe and play independently. During center time, ask the children open-ended questions:

> What do you notice by playing here today?
> What is your favorite part about this center?
> What happens when you make a shadow with your hands close up?
> What happens when you make a shadow with your hands far away?

Math

- Make a shadow-matching game. On posterboard, trace several classroom items, such as scissors, a block, paper clips, and a pencil. Title the posterboard "The Shadow Game." After removing the items, color the tracings a shadowy black. Place the items on a tray and have the children match each item to its shadow.

- To make this matching activity game more challenging, provide items that are quite similar in shape but create shadows of different sizes. For instance, a tall, narrow block lying on its side would cast a long rectangular shadow. However, if the block is standing upright, its shadow would appear as a small square.

- During center time, engage in meaningful discussion with the children by asking open-ended questions:

> How did you find this item's shadow?
> How did you know that this was its shadow?
> What if you laid the object this way—does it still have a shadow?

- Create a math graph using the shelter information families have provided. Title large chart paper "What kind of shelter do you live in?" Include four columns, and label them "apartment," "trailer," "house," and "other." During a group time activity in connection with your burrow shelter for animals, discuss the children's shelter. Place all their responses from home on the chart paper. Afterward, discuss math graph terms, such as *most, least,* and *how many more than.*

Blocks and Building

- Have the children make burrows and denlike sculptures using blocks, snap-block cubes, and other construction items. Provide flashlights for shadow finding and added fun.

Language Arts

- Make an entertaining conjecture book titled *Whose Shadow Is This?* These books are always enjoyable because children get to speculate about which shadow is whose, and the story's predictability helps children feel successful when they independently read it again and again. On the computer, create a page with the question, "Whose shadow is this?" Print out several copies of this page. Next, take a picture of each child. These will be placed on the following pages, which will each read, "It is [child's name]'s shadow." Also trace a simple outline of each child's picture onto black construction paper. To do this, you can simply copy an extra set of pictures, cut out the outline of each child, and trace it onto black construction paper. Glue one outline on each "Whose shadow is this?" page. As you turn to the next page and view each child's picture, the children will enjoy shouting, "It is [child's name]'s shadow." Continue reading until all the children have been included. For added fun, include your own picture on the last page.

  For name-writing practice, allow the children to write their own names on the blank line. For younger children, you can simply write or type their names. After you put the book together, read it with the class and praise the children for their strong reading abilities.

Teacher Reminder: Predictable books are perfect for your emergent readers. The children always enjoy being able to independently read and also treasure viewing each other's pictures.

Reading

- Provide groundhog, ground squirrel, and other rodent books for your reading center. Include nonfiction books about shadows, burrows, and hibernation and fiction books that discuss shadows. Some books you can feature include *Moonbear's Shadow* by Frank Asch and *What Makes a Shadow?* by Clyde Robert Bulla.

- For more shadow fun, include small towels or baby blankets and flashlights for the children to read under. It is always exciting to read a special book while undercover. Remind children to sit upright and be completely safe during their reading time. If you feel the children are too young for towel/blanket reading fun, turn the lights off and have the children sit together and read quietly, using their flashlights.

Writing

- Sequence a groundhog story. I like to include a four-part picture sequence of the groundhog's legendary story on large index cards. On the other side of the index card, you can write *1, 2, 3,* and *4* to indicate the story order. This will help the children to self-assess their sequencing work. Model for the children how to sequence the pictures. Say aloud, "First the groundhog pokes his head out of his burrow. Second, he sees his shadow. Third, the groundhog gets scared and goes back into his burrow. And fourth, the groundhog goes back to sleep for six more weeks of winter." Children can practice sequencing this story independently. By including the text on the cards itself, the children can independently write and illustrate their own groundhog story.

- Include shadow words and outlines on predictable sentence strips for the children to copy and base illustrations on. Begin with simple, predictable sentences:

  This is a pencil's shadow.
  This is a paper clip's shadow.
  This is a pair of scissors' shadow.
  This is a block's shadow.

  At the end of each sentence, include a simple black outline or shadow of the item mentioned. The children can copy these sentences onto blank writing paper and include illustrations beneath their writing.

Dramatic Play

- Create a tunnel-like area in your dramatic play center by using boxes, chairs, and blankets. Provide a flashlight as well. Children can pretend to be groundhogs sleeping underground. They can poke their heads up, flash a light to see their shadows, and then dive back in the burrow and sleep for six more weeks (okay, two minutes!). They will enjoy doing this again and again. Children benefit from taking on the roles of others, especially those who have the power to determine whether there will be six more weeks of winter.

Art

- Make a groundhog puppet. This simple puppet will teach the children about burrows. Here is what you will need:

  Cardboard tissue holder to serve as the burrow
  Large craft stick to be the groundhog
  Green and brown crayons
  Black marker

  Begin by having the children color half the tissue holder green for the grass. For an added dimension, cut strips in the top of the green part and curl the strips with a pencil to make them more grasslike. The other half can be colored brown for the underground burrows. Next, children can color the top third of their craft stick brown, like the furry brown groundhog. Make a face on it, using the black marker. Using the puppet as your prop, tell the sequential story from the writing center activity on page 105.

  "First the groundhog pokes his head out of his burrow." *Poke the craft stick up through the burrow tunnel.*

  "Second, he sees his shadow." *Take stick out and twist it as the groundhog looks around.*

  "Third, the groundhog gets scared and goes back into his burrow." *Quickly poke the craft stick back down through the grassy side entrance.*

  "And fourth, the groundhog goes back to sleep for six more weeks of winter." *Place the stick on its side, sleeping soundly underneath its burrowed shelter.*

  The children can take their puppets home and tell the story to their families.

Music

- Find a shadow song on a teacher-oriented website or in a book. Sing this to the tune of "I'm a Little Teapot":

  I'm a Little Shadow
  I'm a little shadow.
  I'm always a sight.
  I'm with you in the morning, all day, and all night.
  When the sun is out, I'm easy to see.
  Just move your arms and dance with me.

  Then have all the children jump up and dance around with their shadow.

Teacher Reminder:
Use the songs as a transitional activity, such as after cleaning up at your shadow and burrow centers; sing songs during cleanup time. This is a great way to connect thematic ideas to the children's comprehension.

Closing the Groundhogs, Shadows, and Burrows Theme

Throughout your work with the Groundhog, Shadows, and Burrows activities, ask children questions to increase their comprehension. During your group times, be sure to discuss interesting facts they have learned during this theme. Here are some additional questions you can use during activities and to bring this theme to a close:

What is the story of the groundhog?
What have you learned about burrows?
What is a shelter?
Tell me what you have learned about shadows.

Winter Theme 6: Who Are the Hibernators?

Exploring Outside

The winter season provides a sense of stillness, so hibernation and the animals who hibernate can be studied from this perspective. You certainly won't be waking any sleeping animals for your winter hibernating lessons. Don't forget those dormant plants either.

Before you head outdoors on what would be considered a wintry day for your region, discuss the term *hibernation* with the children. Have them slowly sound out each syllable. Provide a simple definition of *hibernation*, such as "dormant" or "sleeping during the winter." Explain how hibernating animals live off their fat and how their breathing slows. Provide some pictures showing hibernating animals, such as bears, ground squirrels, bats, amphibians, and ladybugs. For an even more meaningful connection with the term *hibernation*, explain how in all but the warmest regions, plants go through a state of dormancy in the winter too.

For your Exploring Outside activity, focus on the stillness and quiet of the winter season. On a calm winter day, take a nature hike and notice the gentle air. If you observe any burrows, such as the shelter of a chipmunk or other ground squirrel, point out that the animals are probably hibernating right now. Explain once again that it is best not to get too close so you won't scare any animals. Along your walk, if your notice plants or trees that are dormant, point out the characteristics that are similar to animals' hibernation. Share how plants become temporarily inactive, too, by losing leaves, turning brown, or not flowering.

Hibernating questions and wonder statements can include these:

What type of animal do you think lives in there?
What might the animal be doing right now?
What else do you notice?
I wonder what it looks like while it is hibernating.
I wonder if it dreams.
I wonder if it gets hungry.

For your dormant plant questions, try these:

How does it know when to go dormant?
How will it know when to start growing again?
Why do plants and animals choose winter to be dormant?
What else do you notice?

Role Play Outside

While outdoors, explain to the children that they get to be hibernating animals. Help them get into their choice of hibernating animals by reminding them that hibernating animals breathe very slowly and are also very quiet and still. Have them curl up like sleeping animals, and get them to notice their breath as they slow their breathing. Practice inhaling deeply and exhaling slowly together. Help bring stillness and quiet to the hibernating children by gently repeating, "Shh, I hear only sounds like the gentle, quiet winter wind." Keep the calmness going by reminding them, "You are hibernating animals, sleeping soundly through winter. Your breathing is slow and deep."

After this hibernation role play, ask the children to gently wake up and share with you what it felt like to be the hibernating animal. To generate imaginative dialogue, ask, "Share two important things about your pretend hibernation."

Use open-ended questions and statements to encourage higher-level thinking skills:

How did it feel to pretend to be a hibernating animal?
Tell me what your thoughts were.
What did you look like while you were pretending to hibernate?
How did it feel?

Teacher Reminder:
Try this activity during your naptime schedule. It is sure to calm even your non-nappers.

Involving Families: Studying Hibernating Animals at Home

Supply the children with some fun activities to do at home. Mention the activities in your weekly newsletter to families. Explain to families that the optional activities are provided for extra quality time together in nature and to involve them in their children's education. Explain that the children are learning about hibernating animals. Describe the following nature activities for the families to enjoy at home:

- Tell your families that the children are learning about hibernating animals and that your reading center now features nonfiction and fiction books about bears, bats, amphibians, and other animals that hibernate through winter. Ask families to send in one teddy bear. The children will be able to snuggle up with their teddies and read to their stuffed friends about hibernation. Also tell families that you will be creating many live math graphs with the teddy bears they send (see Reading activity, page 112, and Math activity, page 111). Thank them in advance for all of their help with their children's education.

- Suggest that families visit their local library and choose their own book about hibernating animals and snuggle onto a sofa or bed and read together as if they were hibernating in a den.

Integrating Nature: Studying Hibernating Animals in the Classroom

There is nothing sleepy about this winter theme. Studying hibernating animals is bound to get children interested in role play and involved in these lively centers. As always, young children enjoy any type of theme in which active creatures are the topic of study. When you add mysterious tunnels and burrows, these hideaways become instant favorites too. The following activities incorporate hibernating animals into the areas of science and discovery, math, blocks and building, language arts, reading, writing, dramatic play, art, and music.

Science and Discovery

- Display posters of hibernating animals, such as bears, badgers, bats, frogs, turtles, and snakes. Remind the children that hibernation is a persistent, shallow sleep.

- Share how pulse rates slow for hibernating animals. Provide stethoscopes, and show the children how to listen to one another's heart rate. Show them how to feel one another's pulse rate as well. Allow the children to independently observe and play.

- During center time, engage in meaningful dialogue with the children by asking open-ended questions:

What do you notice by playing here today?
What is your favorite part of this center?
What do you notice about your friend's heart beat/pulse?

Math

- Connect your Science activity to this math center by creating a sorting/classifying activity. Make a poster with three headings: "Hibernate," "Migrate," and "Adapt." Include pictures of all three types of animals on index cards: animals that migrate, those that hibernate, and those that adapt. Review in simple terms with the children these three different types of animals. *Migrate* means to move from one place to another. *Hibernation* means to go into a dormant sleep. And *adapt* refers to adjusting to the situation or environment—for example, growing thicker hair when it gets colder or changing color to blend in with one's surroundings and avoid being hurt or eaten.

  Allow the children to sort and classify the index card pictures under "Migrate," "Hibernate," or "Adapt." During center time, ask meaningful questions of the children:

  What does *hibernate* mean?
  What does it mean to migrate/adapt?
  Why did you put the pictures where you put them?
  Which type of animal would you like to be?

- Create a large, interactive teddy bear graph. Using the teddy bears that the children brought from home, create two-column graphs. Focus on a two-variable attribute by making two columns. For instance, your first teddy bear columns may include teddy bears that have bows and those that do not. Or sort teddy bears that are black from those that are not. You can classify and sort by large teddy bears and all other teddy bear sizes, by small teddy bears and all other ones. Each time, develop the children's higher-level math logic by asking them, "How did I sort them this time?" After each graph, discuss such math graph terms as *most, least,* and *how many more than.*

Blocks and Building

- Have the children make burrows and caves using blocks, snap-block cubes, and other construction items. Include little toy animals they can use for more hibernating fun.

Language Arts

- Make a large chart about all the different hibernating animals. Your chart might include grizzly bears, brown and black bears, groundhogs, possums, skunks, marmots, badgers, frogs, snakes, turtles, and other amphibians. Include simple stick drawings for your early readers.

- Use your chart information to make a predictable classroom book, *Who Are the Hibernators?* On the computer, print a page that reads "A ____ hibernates." Print several copies. Next, have the children each pick an animal from the chart to illustrate. More advanced children can phonetically write the name of their animal on the blank line. Have the younger children dictate their responses so you can write the animal's name in the blank. To conclude your nonfiction classroom big book, provide a semi-unpredictable ending to your predictable piece. Take a picture of the entire class and include it on the last page, which should read, "Humans do NOT hibernate." Bind it with three rings or string, and read the book to the entire class. Children will love to see their contribution.

- Afterward, place your predictable book in your reading center for all to enjoy again and again.

Reading

- Provide hibernation books for your reading center. Include books on bears, bats, amphibians, and other animals that hibernate through winter. Some books you can feature include *The Valentine Bears* by Eve Bunting, *Sleep, Big Bear, Sleep* by Maureen Wright, and *Hibernation* by Anita Ganeri.

- Include the language arts activity's *Who Are the Hibernators?* predictable book in the reading center for children to revisit when they wish.

- Include the teddy bears that children have brought from home in your reading area for them to snuggle up and read with.

- For added fun, create a cavelike entryway to your reading area, using large boxes and blankets. Children can pretend they are getting ready for their long winter's nap by reading a few books with their teddies from home.

Teacher Reminder:
Predictable books are perfect for your emergent readers, while the semi-unpredictable ending provides a challenge for your more advanced readers. The children always enjoy the satisfaction of being able to read independently and also admire viewing each other's illustrations.

Writing

- Connect your writing center to your language arts activity by using the *Who Are the Hibernators?* book as a reference for making predictable sentence strips. Have the children dictate and illustrate more hibernation pictures. Begin with simple, predictable sentences:

  A bear hibernates.
  A groundhog hibernates.
  A turtle hibernates.
  A bat hibernates.

  After each animal word, include a picture of that animal to help your emergent readers and writers. The children can copy these sentences onto blank writing paper and draw illustrations below their sentences.

Dramatic Play

- You cannot have a hibernating theme without the classic tale "Goldilocks and the Three Bears." Set up your dramatic play area to include three sizes of bowls and spoons, chairs, and sleeping bags. Children will enjoy the drama of the wee little bowl, the just-right chair, and the too-big sleeping bag. Children will delight in this story during your "Who Are the Hibernators?" theme.

Art

- Teach children that bears need to fill up their bellies before going into their deep sleep. Have fun learning this new fact by discussing what bears eat. Tell the children that today they will fill up their own human bellies with this fun art activity. Have children put paint smocks on. Here is what you will need for this yummy art activity:

  Fingerpaint paper cut into a bear shape
  Chocolate pudding to paint and create a colorful chocolate brown bear
  Plastic spoons and paper cups

  Begin by giving each child a paper bear shape. Give each child a plastic spoon and a paper cup full of chocolate pudding. Allow the children to dollop a spoonful of pudding onto their papers and swirl away.

Spice up this art activity by connecting it to the language arts activity from page 112. Include bear words on chart paper, and allow the children to practice writing them with fingers on their pudding-filled paper. Be sure to include pictures on your chart paper too: grizzly bear, polar bear, brown bear, black bear, and panda bear.

When the children are finished with their creations, they can fill up their bellies with the remaining pudding.

Music

- Sing a hibernation song you've found in a book or online. Here is a song you can sing to the tune of the children's classic "Frère Jacques." Begin by telling all the children to curl up and hibernate.

Are You Hibernating?
Are you hibernating,
Are you hibernating,
Grizzly Bear?
Groundhog and Possum?
It is almost springtime.
It is almost springtime.
Stretch and wake up.
Stretch and wake up.

Then have all the children stretch, yawn, and move slowly.

For the second verse, replace *grizzly bear* with *brown* and *black bear*, replace *groundhog* and *possum* with *skunks* and *marmots*. Certainly you could add more verses by including many more hibernating animals. When finished, ask the children to say which hibernating animal they chose to be.

Teacher Reminder:
Using songs as a transitional activity, such as after cleaning up your "Who Are the Hibernators?" centers, is a great way to add more thematic connection and to enhance the children's comprehension.

Closing the Who Are the Hibernators? Theme

Throughout your work with the "Who Are the Hibernators?" activities, ask children questions to increase their comprehension. During your group times, be sure to discuss interesting facts they've learned about hibernating animals. Here are some additional questions you can use during activities and to bring this theme to a close:

What have you learned about hibernation?
When do animals hibernate?
What are some of your favorite hibernating animals?

Winter Theme 7: What's the Weather?

Exploring Outside

Toward the end of winter, cabin fever can affect the best of us. It is time to get outside, regardless of the weather, and introduce the idea of meteorology to the classroom. For your "What's the Weather?" outside exploration, you may want to choose several days with different types of weather to get outside and observe. Whether you live north or south, east or west, the winter season is sure to bring a full array of weather just outside your classroom.

Explain to the children that they will become weather experts, also known as meteorologists. Discuss the term *meteorology* with the children. Keep it simple as you share the basics. Although *meteorology* is technically the study of the earth's atmosphere, you can discuss it with your youngsters as the science of weather. *Meteorologist* stems from the Greek word *meteoron*, meaning "high in the sky."

When you're all outdoors, remind children that just because snow or rain is on the ground does not mean it is snowing or raining. Rather, their meteorologists' eyes should look high in the sky to determine the weather.

Ask open-ended questions, such as these:

What do you notice?
What type of weather do you think will happen today?
What else do you notice?

The children's responses may once again generate other questions and discussion topics.

Role Play Outside

While outdoors, explain to the children that they get to be the weather. Ask them what type of weather they are. Are they snowy, rainy, foggy, cloudy, or sunny? Help suggest options for them to try out many weather roles. Encourage the children to use "I" terms when they describe two important things about themselves. When you ask them to be specific and to identify two important things about themselves, they bring essential points to their language and thinking and develop better understanding of the critical attributes of weather as well.

Continue asking the children to say more about themselves. Using the statement, "Tell me about yourself!" helps initiate imaginative thinking and creative talk. Other effective open-ended questions include these:

> What are you doing today? Why?
> How long can you do this?
> Where will you go when you are finished?
> What do you think you will be tomorrow?
> What do you look like?
> What do you like about yourself?

Involving Families: Studying Weather at Home

Supply the children with some fun activities to do at home. Mention the activities in your weekly newsletter to families. Explain to families that the optional activities are provided for extra quality time together in nature and to involve them in their children's education. Explain that the children are learning about the weather and all its attributes. Describe the following nature activities for the families to enjoy at home.

- Send home a sheet that reads, "Our family likes to ____ on a rainy day." Be sure there is also a space above for the family name and a sentence below inviting them to draw a picture of the activity. Ask families to fill in the blank and have their child illustrate a "rainy day picture." Later tell families how much you appreciate their contribution and how it helped to create a *Rainy Day Family Activities Book* for the classroom.

- Remind families that children do not need to watch the news and should be shielded from many of its shocking segments. However, the weather portion can certainly be viewed. Explain that if the children are in the other room playing while the news is on, they should call them in to view the weather forecast for the week together. The little ones will be able to practice some of their new vocabulary from their meteorology fun in the classroom.

Integrating Nature: Studying Weather in the Classroom

As the end of winter approaches and spring starts to appear, "What's the Weather?" is the perfect theme for this transitional time in the seasons. Will it be rainy or snowy? Warmer or colder than usual? It doesn't matter; the more unpredictable the weather, the better! Even if the weather is humdrum, not to worry—the children will bring their positive attitudes to these exciting weather and meteorology activities.

Science and Discovery

- Display posters showing different types of weather. Including pictures of each season will help the children's weather comprehension.

- Include an assortment of thermometers. During center time, put out three bowls of water, one very warm, one room temperature, and one icy cold. Children will be able to compare and contrast thermometers and water temperatures.

- Using two empty two-liter bottles, create a waterfall tornado by filling one of the bottles three-quarters full. Connect the empty bottle with a tornado tube (which can be bought from any science, teacher supply, or toy store, or better yet, borrowed from a colleague or science teacher) and turn it upside down. Give a swirly, twisty motion, and the children will enjoy watching the water naturally flow into a twister. Add blue food coloring and sparkles for a mesmerizing experience. Although the technical name for this water activity is a *vortex*, children tend to refer to it as the "waterfall tornado."

- Have some fun with weather water exploration. Begin by placing some objects in a large tub of water to become frozen treasures. I like to put plastic toy fish in the water, but small items such as a plastic cup or other toys will work too. Place the tub in the freezer for a day or two. When the water is fully frozen, unload the large frozen cube into a water table. Off to one side, place a small bowl of warm water, eyedroppers, and small measuring cups. Allow the

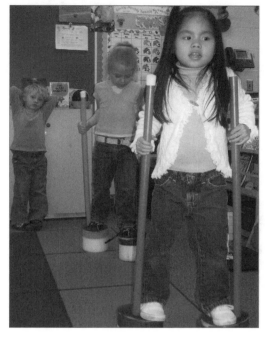

Abby and Faith practice their large-motor skills by pretending to walk through puddles with puddle walkers.

Abby and Tim watch a vortex flow downward in the tornado tube.

These children unthaw frozen items in the water and then continue with their water play.

children to drop the warm water onto the large frozen cube. Eventually they will find the frozen treasure items when the water melts. As the ice thaws, be sure to include beakers and measuring cups for more water fun.

Engage in meaningful conversation with the children by asking open-ended questions:

What are you doing here today?
What do you notice?
What else did you discover?

Math

- Create a daily weather graph. Title a piece of large chart paper "What's the weather today?" Below the heading, list some typical weather words for your region at this particular time of year. For example, you may want to include s*nowy, cloudy, sunny,* and *rainy.* Each day, pick a child to be the weather watcher. He can go to the window with a set of binoculars and come back with the weather forecast. (If you do not have binoculars, staple two cardboard tissue holders together for the children to look through.) If she says "sunny," make a check in the sunny column. Continue each day until all the children have had a turn at being the weather watcher. Then discuss the graph and the terms *most, least,* and *how many more than.*

- See also the music activity, pages 121–22, which has a strong math connection.

Blocks and Building

- It is important to revisit past lessons to reinforce children's comprehension. Notice this time that there's an added twist to this favorite Blocks and Building activity. Remind the children about the term *shelter,* which you used during the Coniferous Tree theme. This time, focus on how shelter keeps us safe from the wind, rain, snow, and other weather elements. Talk about all the types of homes we live in that provide safe shelter for all of us. Be sure to mention apartments, trailers, houses, and temporary shelters, such as tents, huts, and lean-tos. Once again, encourage children to create all of the types of shelters using the blocks. When the children share their creations with you, praise them, using the review vocabulary word *shelter* and saying, "That shelter is awesome! It looks like it would keep a family warm and cozy."

Language Arts

- Let your budding meteorologists practice their speaking skills on TV. Take a large box, cut out a large hole in the bottom for the screen's opening, and cover the entire box with brown construction paper or paper bags. Make an antenna for the top by covering a paper bowl in foil for the base and taping foiled pipe cleaners to the base to be the rabbit ears. Add knobs by hot-gluing drink tops beneath the TV screen.

  Add these cutout construction paper call letters: W-Pre-K TV. Include a toy microphone, or make one by molding an aluminum foil ball over the top of an empty tissue tube holder. Model for the children how to act as the meteorologist: "Welcome to W-Pre-K TV. The weather today is cold. Get out those warm coats, hats, and mittens. You will need to dress for the weather. It looks as though there is going to be snow in the air. Check back later for tomorrow's weather. We are hoping for some sunny skies soon. Have your sunglasses ready as the snow starts to disappear."

  The children will love being meteorologists. You will have many of them wanting to be meteorologists, so here is a helpful hint: create a checklist with all of the children's names on it. At the top, write "Did you get to be a meteorologist?" Include tally marks to keep track of who has held this popular role.

Catrice is the meteorologist today and shares what her weather predictions are.

Reading

- Collect the "Our family likes to ____ on a rainy day" sheets that families completed and returned (see Involving Families, page 116). Add a cover page, "Our Class's Rainy Day Activities," and staple or bind the pages together. Read the book to the children. Afterward, include the homemade book in your reading center.

- Provide different types of weather books in your reading center for children to explore. Include fiction. Some books you can feature include *Cloudy with a Chance of Meatballs* by Judi Barrett and *Rain Talk* by Mary Serfozo.

- Be sure to feature your special homemade *Rainy Day Activities* book from the families too.

- Keep the TV from the Literary Arts activity in your reading center. Children can sit back and pretend to read the weather from the newspaper while watching the weatherperson on the television screen.

Writing

- Include writing tools and printed 8½ x 11 inch paper at your writing center that reads "I like to play in the ____." Have nearby some sentence strips with such weather words as *sun, snow,* and *rain,* and pictures corresponding on them. The children can refer to the sentence strips to fill in the blank on the full sheet of paper, creating the sentences they prefer. For example:

  I like to play in the sun.
  I like to play in the snow.
  I like to play in the rain.

The children can illustrate their weather word below the sentence.

Dramatic Play

- Add a pair of binoculars and plenty of seasonal gear to the dramatic play center. Bring in snow pants, heavy coats and winter boots, raincoats and puddle boots with an umbrella, and even sunglasses and sandals. (Hint: there are probably heaps of these items in lost and found.)
  The children can look out the window with their binoculars and predictably decide, "Should I wear snow pants and a winter jacket?" or "Maybe I should put on my raincoat and puddle boots," or "Will I need an umbrella today?" If they are really lucky, maybe they'll just add sandals and sunglasses to the smart outfits they already have on. Regardless of the weather, children will enjoy trying on clothing for their winter or spring role.

Art

- Make abstract cumulus cloud prints. Here is what you will need to make them:

  > Large fingerpaint paper cutouts in the shape of puffy cumulus clouds
  > Shaving cream, preferably the type for sensitive skin
  > Blue food coloring

  Have the children wear their paint smocks for this activity. At an art table, give a small group of children a handful of shaving cream. Allow them to spread the shaving cream in their area of the table. They can imagine pictures in the cumulus clouds, such as boats and rabbits, cats, and ice cream cones. They can continue making all sorts of creations in their shaving cream (which I refer to as "puffy white cumulus cloud cream"), just as clouds change and look like different pictures over time.

  When the shaving cream begins to lose its thick, creamy texture, add just a drop of blue coloring. Instruct the children to now make the one picture they would like to capture. When they have finished their shaving cream picture on the table, gently place the shiny side of the fingerpaint paper facedown on the cream, and then lift it up to view the abstract cumulus cloud print. When the prints are dry, write on the paper what the children said they saw in their cumulus clouds, such as a rabbit or pirate. This is a fun activity for the children. Because you used "puffy white cumulus cloud cream" instead of fingerpaint, the fingerpaint paper will not curl. It will dry so the children can hang their clouds high in the sky in their bedrooms at home.

Music

- Here is a song I devised to help the children understand the nature of puffy white cumulus clouds and to aid in their early math skills. Use a felt board and ten white felt cumulus clouds at your music center. The children will be able to practice counting, using one-to-one correspondence while singing this song. As you sing the first verse, invite the children to add one felt cloud at a time to the board. When you sing it backwards, invite the children to remove one felt cloud at a time from the board. Sing "One Little, Two Little, Three Little Cumulus Clouds" to the tune of "One Little, Two Little, Three Little Indians":

One Little, Two Little, Three Little Cumulus Clouds
One little, two little, three little cumulus clouds,
four little, five little, six little cumulus clouds,
seven little, eight little, nine little cumulus clouds,
ten little cumulus clouds floating in the sky.

Ten little, nine little, eight little cumulus clouds,
seven little, six little, five little cumulus clouds,
four little, three little, two little cumulus clouds,
one little cumulus cloud floating in the sky.

Closing the What's the Weather? Theme

Throughout your work with the "What's the Weather?" activities, ask children questions to increase their comprehension. During your group times, be sure to discuss all of the different types of weather. Here are some additional questions you can use during activities and to bring this theme to a close:

What have you learned about the weather?
What is a meteorologist?
What have you noticed about the weather today?
What is your favorite weather and why?

Spring Nature Study
March, April, May

Spring Reading List

Here is a list of the books I recommend providing the children throughout the spring themes:

Anthony, Joseph P. *The Dandelion Seed.*
Brown, Marcia. *Stone Soup.*
Christian, Peggy. *If You Find a Rock.*
Florian, Douglas. *Handsprings.*
Glaser, Linda. *It's Spring.*
Gibbons, Gail. *Frogs.*
————. *From Seed to Plant.*
Heller, Ruth. *Chickens Aren't the Only Ones.*
Krauss, Ruth. *The Carrot Seed.*
Lionni, Leo. *An Extraordinary Egg.*
Polacco, Patricia. *Rechenka's Eggs.*
Posada, Mia. *Dandelions: Stars in the Grass.*
Singer, Marilyn. *How to Cross a Pond: Poems About Water.*
Waters, Jennifer. *Spring Has Sprung.*

Marveling at New Life and Growth

By being truly aware of the shift to spring, regardless of where you live, it becomes the most hopeful season. Everywhere, new life is happening: birds are hatching, buds are forming, and plants are emerging from dirt. Spring is full of promise and assurance. This season's themes address many of spring's characteristics, such as emerging new life, budding surprises, and growing animal and plant forms. It is the transition from winter to summer, the change from cold to a bit warmer temperatures. This miraculous time of year focuses on hope and new existence, promising life and growth. As buds appear in the spring, we can reflect on our own lives and see where we would like to naturally blossom as well. Spring enlightens us by showing us how to emerge into our own uniqueness. It is a fine season to renew the spirit and to help children discover more of who they are as well.

My Spring Reflection

Spring is the perfect time to ward off the end-of-winter blues and any existing cabin fever. Bring along your new spring attitude and a fresh outlook to the season. Spring is the time to investigate the new life in front of you.

Flowers come to my mind when I reflect on childhood in spring. I picked dandelion bouquets for my mom. "Close your eyes!" I'd say, holding up my gift of beautifully droopy dandelions. Mom smiled and made them the centerpiece of our table.

Once spring arrived, our family's yard quickly filled with bikes, Frisbees, horseshoes, lawn darts, and sidewalk chalk. The neighborhood kids knew where to play, and our yard became covered with every outdoor plaything known to children. Our lawn had more than its share of dirt mounds with an overabundance of toy cars and tractors, and forks and spoons for digging and path making.

The neighbors next door had a perfect lawn. It was staked off with natural twine and had flawless grass with no weeds. One spring afternoon, I stepped over that twine fence and walked directly to the neighbor's side yard, where beautiful red spring flowers grew below their kitchen window. I picked every bright red tulip. I thought my mom would love these flowers. I put them behind my back and excitedly walked into our kitchen and told her to close her eyes. When she opened them this time, she turned pale and held herself up against the stove. We nervously walked to the neighbor's house, explained what had happened, and handed the bright red bouquet to our neighbor. She empathized and kindly ended the conversation by handing my mother one brilliant red tulip. Mom thanked her, and as we walked home hand in hand, mom gave me the special-flowers-that-you-don't-pick lecture.

I was moved by the beauty of nature, awed by its perfection, and amazed by the magnificence of flowers. I was drawn to them for nourishment, just like nature's hummingbird or honeybee. When I handed others a flower or a bouquet of weeds, I felt the amazing power of making people smile.

Your Spring Reflection

What moves you about this season? What particular spring attributes are you drawn to? What important new life questions come to you this spring? Let's get right into the season of investigating new life and the inspiring weeks ahead. Here is a teacher reflection for you to use during this promising new season. Once again, as you begin each season, use the reflection as a beginning balancing point for your own sense of appreciation of the season in front of you. This gratitude and appreciation for nature is a superb place to take in nature and all the newness spring has to offer. Reflection is always a helpful balancing source to use when working with little ones. It strengthens your emotional, spiritual, and intellectual dimensions. It is a healthy excercise you can use with all the seasons.

What spring story from your childhood comes to your mind? Which stories will you share with the children? This is another opportunity for you to bring spring and all the new life it has to offer to the young minds in front of you. Storytelling always provides appreciation for nature on another level and encourages the children to get outdoors and create their own memorable new life spring stories!

Here are some lists and questions to ponder as the current season enters your spirit and classroom.

What does spring mean to you?

_____

_____

_____

_____

What has this season meant to you in the past?

_____

_____

_____

_____

_____

When reminiscing, what past stories come to your mind?

_____

_____

_____

_____

_____

How will you personally take time to enjoy this season?

_____

_____

_____

_____

_____

What are you thankful for this spring season?

_____

_____

_____

_____

_____

How will you set the tone for the season ahead?

_____

_____

_____

_____

_____

Are there any special activities you can include to bring in the season in your own way?

_____

_____

_____

_____

_____

_____

Sing in the Season

Begin the season with a song saying good-bye to the season you have just finished and welcoming the season ahead. By continuing to do this with all the seasons, you help children strengthen their predictive skills. By the end of the year, the children will say, "Let's sing the good-bye–hello song!" Praise them for their strong memory skills. All of this gives the children a simple ritual for saying good-bye to the season they have just enjoyed and helps them appreciate the newness of the season with all of its budding surprises. Building that healthy sense of saying good-bye, letting go, and surrendering to what is in front of us is another wonderful skill that nature can teach us. Sing "Good-bye, Winter! Hello, Spring!" to the tune of "Good Night, Ladies":

Good-Bye, Winter! Hello, Spring!
Good-bye, winter; good-bye, winter; good-bye, winter;
We enjoyed you so!

Hello, spring; hello, spring; hello, spring;
We welcome you right now!

Invite Families to Participate

Help families join their children in noticing spring signs and investigating new life. Send home a brief letter to families to introduce your upcoming nature activities for spring. Remember—you are helping tremendously by including families in your getting-children-outdoors mission and wholesome environment education. Ask families to provide pictures and spring signs, such as flowers, buds, new leaves, or anything else that will bring the spring topic to curious young minds. Here is a sample introductory letter to send home:

Dear Families,

Happy almost spring! In preparing for the upcoming spring season in our classroom, we will be asking for your help in the weeks ahead. The children will soon be delving into these spring topics at school:

- Water Sources
- First Flowers
- Oviparous Animals
- Miraculous Seeds
- Tadpoles to Frogs
- Dandy Dandelions
- Finding Stones

Be on the lookout this spring for our simple nature homework activities. These will all be wholesome, fun family activities that will provide enjoyment for the season, such as taking a walk in nature, looking for first spring flowers, showing respect to animals, and noticing other spring attributes. In the meantime, please send a simple spring treasure with your child to school. These will be added to our Spring Family Treasures box. Items can include such things as a picture of a fun family spring activity or a flower blossom you have found during the spring season. We will be discussing these individual items during our group circle time. Our group time discussions will enhance the children's listening, speaking, reading, and writing skills and provide an opportunity to integrate the seasonal theme in all of their learning.

Thank you in advance for all your spring contributions. More important, thank you for your involvement in your child's education! As a side note, you are probably well aware that today's children need more time outdoors enjoying nature. They need time to appreciate the simple things our environment has to offer. I value having you join me in helping with this important task.

Here's to celebrating the spring season and all of its new gifts.

My best to you,
[insert your signature here]

Decorate a shoe box or other box with spring-looking construction paper and decorations. Be as creative as you wish. Label the box "Spring Family Treasures." When the children bring their treasure items to school, have them put the items in the spring treasure chest. Later let each child talk about the items during your group meeting time.

In your weekly newsletters, remind families of any specific requests this season, such as drinking water with their child and talking about how it helps our bodies, or looking for flowering trees this spring. In the newsletter, also mention the upcoming optional home activities that are created to help families and their children connect with nature and all its richness.

Spring Theme 1: Water Sources

Exploring Outside

Take the children to a natural water source outdoors. Perhaps a brook is nearby, or some larger puddles on the school grounds. Certainly a human-made channel, such as a trough or drain, would work as well. Visiting several water sources in the vicinity provides a perfect opportunity to compare and contrast. Allow the children to freely explore the water with sticks and their fingers.

Ask open-ended questions to encourage creative thinking and to help children examine nature's life more closely:

What is happening with the water?
Why are there crinkles and ridges in the frozen part?
What else do you see?
What does the water sound like?
When you hold up a frozen piece, what does it look like?
What else do you notice?

Role Play Outside

While outdoors, explain to the children that they get to be water. Ask them to move like water and make sounds like it. Children should use "I" terms when describing themselves while pretending to be water. Begin by encouraging them: "Let me hear what you sound like." The potential for questions is endless.

Be sure to ask open-ended questions to help children develop higher-level thinking skills. Use questions like these:

What do you look like?
How did you get here?
What do you like about yourself?
How do you help our earth?

Involving Families: Studying Water at Home

Supply the children with some fun activities to do at home. Mention the activities in your weekly newsletter to families. Explain to families that the optional activities are provided for extra quality time together in nature and to involve them in their children's education. Explain that the children are learning about the precious resource water. Share the following nature activities for the families to enjoy at home:

- Suggest that each family member drink a glass of water with a meal. They can also talk about why water is important for our bodies.

- Remind families to turn off the water when brushing their teeth. Explain the importance of conserving water so they can talk about it at home.

- Families can play outside and find water to observe around the home. Adults can ask the children to share their observations.

Integrating Nature: Studying Water in the Classroom

Bring a bucket of the water from your Exploring Outside trek back to use in the classroom's integrative centers. You can keep the water in the bucket for now or pour it into a dish tub, large bin, water table, or sink. If need be, you can discreetly add some faucet water to your spring water for some of the activities. However, there is no need to point this out to the children. It is more important for them to understand that water was brought from an outdoor source back to the classroom for their exploration and to use in some of the following activities.

Science and Discovery
- Allow a small group of children to continue their water exploration in a water table or large bin. Provide them with eyedroppers, beakers, and magnifying glasses for further scientific discovery.

- Encourage children to draw pictures of what they did in the science and discovery center. Help them write a title for the pictures they've drawn.

- To expand the children's water table exploration, intermittently add frozen cubes during center time.

Math

- Include different sizes of measuring cups for the children to measure and estimate independently. Ask them how many smaller cups it will take to fill a larger container.

- For added fun, provide tall, skinny beakers and short, wide containers for more investigation.

Blocks and Building

- Magical wishes go along with this spring water theme. Turn your blocks and building center into a water wishing well center. Hang up pictures of old-fashioned wells for your young engineers' reference. Provide pennies in a cup too. After the children cooperatively design a unique wishing well, show them how to hold a penny in their hands, close their eyes, make a wish, and toss the penny into the wishing well.

Language Arts

- As a large group, create a diamante poem, "Spring's Water." Diamante poems are great for teaching about connected or opposite things, such as ice and water, sun and moon, bee and flower, or dirt and rock. Here is a simple format I use for creating a diamante poem:

    Line 1: The subject (noun)
    Line 2: Two describing words (adjectives) for Line 1 (the subject)
    Line 3: Three -ing words (participles) describing Line 1
    Line 4: Two nouns that connect with Line 1 and two nouns that connect with line 7
    Line 5: Three -ing words describing line 7
    Line 6: Two describing words (adjectives) for Line 7 (the subject)
    Line 7: The subject (noun)

    Start this diamante poem using the words *Ice* at the top and *Water* at the bottom. Ask the children to suggest words to include in between. Here is an example:

Spring's Water

Ice

Cold   Frosty

Freezing   Cooling   Chilling

Rink   Cubes   Pool   Drink

Thawing   Soaking   Drinking

Clear   Wet

Water

Reading

- Provide books about water for your reading center. Include books on rainwater, drinking water, and activities that make water a necessity: for example, swimming, bathing, water skiing, and boating. Fiction books should be provided as well. Some books you can feature include *How to Cross a Pond: Poems About Water* by Marilyn Singer and *Spring Has Sprung* by Jennifer Waters.

- Include pitchers of water and paper cups so the children can enjoy a drink of water as they read about this precious resource. Children will appreciate water as never before.

Writing

- On sentence strips, write sentences that end with the word *water*. Highlight the word *water* in a different color, such as blue, to encourage children's word recognition and one-to-one word reading correspondence. Including pictures helps children with their early reading skills. Allow the children to write and create independently at the literacy station. For the strips, include these sentences and others:

  I drink water.
  I take a bath in water.
  I brush my teeth with water.

Dramatic Play

- Turn your dramatic play center into a spa and teach children about the healing benefits of water. Bring in scented soaps, bath scrunchies, big bath towels, and washcloths (or ask for donations of these items in your weekly newsletter or via e-mail messages to your colleagues) and place them in wicker baskets. If possible, also include shower caps, eye pillows, bathrobes, slippers, and small lounge chairs. Provide small pitchers of water with cucumber and lemon slices along with paper cups on a decorative mat. Model how to sit back, relax, and enjoy some flavorful water. As you demonstrate, be sure to say soothingly as you sip your water, "Ahh, a glass of healthy water feels so good while I relax." Children can also put warm washcloths on their foreheads as they sit back and take it easy.

Art

- Allow the children to paint with watercolors. Model the importance of using water to rinse the brush each time you change paint colors. Show what happens when you blend the different colors together on paper. Share how water helps the paint to extend further onto the paper.

Music

- Provide a rain stick instrument for children to use independently.

- As a group, perform music and sing songs that refer to water, such as "Rain, Rain, Go Away" and "Eensy Weensy Spider."

Closing the Water Sources Theme

Throughout your work with spring's Water Sources activities, ask children questions to further enhance their comprehension. During your group times, be sure to discuss why we need to be a good partner with nature, focusing specifically on water. Here are some additional questions you can use during activities and to bring this theme to a close:

Why is water important?
Why do you think we should never pollute the water?
Why do people and animals need water?

Spring Theme 2: First Flowers

Exploring Outside

Take the children on a spring walk to look for the first blossoms of the season. Look for flowering trees and the spring's ground flowers. When they've found some, allow the children to closely look at the buds and blossoms.

Ask creative, open-ended questions to encourage the children to examine nature's flowers more closely:

What do you see inside the flower?
What do you notice underneath the petals?
What else do you see?
What does the flower smell like?
What does it feel like?
What else do you notice?

Teacher Reminder: Remind children about the delicacy of flowers to help them develop respect and admiration for nature.

Role Play Outside

While outdoors, explain to the children that they get to be spring flowers. Ask them to show you their beauty. Begin by saying, "Show me your spring splendor." Remind children to use "I" terms when responding during role play. This helps them with identification and language skills.

Statements such as "Tell me about yourself!" always stimulate a fine opening and imaginative dialogue. Afterward, begin using open-ended questions for higher-level thinking development:

What do you look like?
How did you get here?
What do you like about yourself?
What is your purpose on Earth? Tell me more about you!

Take the children outdoors to view spring buds. Be prepared for lively questions and motivating observations!

Involving Families: Studying First Flowers at Home

Supply the children with some fun activities to do at home. Mention the activities in your weekly newsletter to families. Explain to families that the optional activities are provided for extra quality time together in nature and to involve them in their children's education. Explain that the children are learning about the first flowers of spring. Describe the following nature activities for the families to enjoy at home:

- Invite families to take a spring walk and see how many flowering trees and ground flowers they can identify together.

- Propose that families plant the perennial flower mixture that the children will create during the science and discovery activity (below), or give it as a gift to a family, friend, or neighbor who will appreciate and nurture its growth.

Integrating Nature: Studying First Flowers in the Classroom

Bring a few flower specimens back to the classroom for further investigation. Allow each child to pick one favorite flower to bring back as well. Keep the flowers in vases to use in some of the integrative centers. The children will be observing them in your science and discovery center, singing about them in the music center, and writing about the different types of flowers in your writing center. This flower theme is sure to be a delightfully scented good time.

Science and Discovery

- Include large pictures or posters of spring flowers in your science and discovery center. Daffodils, crocuses, and tulips make wonderful spring pictures that can also be used later for reference in the reading and writing centers. Provide three flower vases, one for each variety of flowers. Provide magnifying glasses so the children can examine them more closely. Ask about each flower's similarities and differences. Allow children to explore independently.

- Using peat pots and a perennial flower seed mixture, allow the children to plant seeds and watch them germinate over the next few days and weeks. Afterward, send the flowerpots home for families either to plant or to give as gifts.

Math

- Include measuring instruments, such as rulers, tapes, snap-block cubes, or blocks for independent measuring and estimating. Ask children to measure the length of the flowers' stems. Ask which one is longer or shorter. Also ask about the number of leaves, petals, and other parts.

Blocks and Building

- Make rectangular flower beds in your block area. Direct children's focus to the rectangle shape of the flower beds. They can use blocks to design beautiful rectangular flower beds, add packing peanut soil, and top off their creations by planting a rainbow of spring flowers. Provide silk flowers, garden gloves, and play shovels in your block and building center.

Language Arts

- Make a predictable counting and reading book titled *There Are Flowers in the Garden*. Have children look at the flowers or posters in the science center for reference. Then they can each draw a colored picture of a flower for the book, choosing to make a red, orange, yellow, blue, or purple flower. Each child will create a specified colored flower with her signature underneath. When you insert each child's creation into the big book, be sure everyone signs below his or her drawing.

  Set up the pages on your computer so each page begins with this text: "There are [number] [color] flowers in the garden." Allow older children to phonetically spell out and write the sentence, and include the computer printed text to aid their reading comprehension. For younger children, type and print out the pages with the full sentences shown below. Next, model how to write the numbers 1 through 10 on large chart paper. Children can practice writing these in the air while the teacher models each number correctly.

  Next, write *red, orange, yellow, blue,* and *purple* in the corresponding color. When the children are writing the numbers and colors of their flowers on the page, they can look at the chart paper for extra help and guidance. Include crayons whose labels list the colors *red, orange, yellow, blue,* and *purple.* Children can look at these when writing the color name on their paper; doing so will aid the children's emergent writing skills.

Here's how the book's pages read and how you can use them when you read the book with the children:

There is 1 red flower in the garden. *[As a group, count the flowers.]*

There are 2 orange flowers in the garden. *[As a group, count the flowers.]*

There are 3 yellow flowers in the garden. *[As a group, count the flowers.]*

There are 4 blue flowers in the garden. *[As a group, count the flowers.]*

There are 5 purple flowers in the garden. *[As a group, count the flowers.]*

There is 1 red flower and 5 orange flowers in the garden. *[This time count, and afterward ask: 1 + 5 = What number?]*

There is 1 blue flower and 6 purple flowers in the garden. *[This time count, and afterward ask: 1 + 6 = What number?]*

There is 1 yellow flower and 7 red flowers in the garden. *[This time count, and afterward ask: 1 + 7 = What number?]*

There is 1 orange flower and 8 yellow flowers in the garden. *[This time count, and afterward ask: 1 + 8 = What number?]*

There are 10 beautiful flowers in the garden.

Make sure there are ten flowers by counting them together as a group. As a bonus, include two each of red, orange, yellow, blue, and purple flowers. This time, count again using one-to-one correspondence. Afterward, practice counting by twos.

Children will enjoy reading this book again and again in your reading center. They will be proud they can read their personalized book and view their beautiful illustrations.

Reading

- Provide nonfiction books about many types of flowers. Make sure plenty of the books show colorful close-ups of parts of flowers, such as leaves, petals, sepals, stamens, and pistils. Fiction books should be provided as well. Some books you can feature include *It's Spring* by Linda Glaser and *Handsprings* by Douglas Florian.

- Make your reading center a flowery, aromatic place to enjoy a good book. Include vases of pretty flowers for the children to look at, smell, and take pleasure in as they read about flowers and flowering trees. Children will enjoy sitting back and smelling the roses (or tulips, or crocuses, or other spring flowers) while reading these books. (As always, be mindful of allergies.)

Writing

- Just as you used flowers and posters in your science center, do so in your writing center too. Allow the children to write and create independently at this literacy station. On sentence strips, write sentences that end with the word *flower*. To encourage early word recognition, write the word *flower* in a different color. Consider including pictures for those children with emergent reading skills. Here are some sample sentences you can use:

  A daffodil is a spring flower.
  A tulip is a spring flower.
  A crocus is a spring flower.

Dramatic Play

- Turn your dramatic play center into a garden center. Include play shovels and hoes. Set out an abundance of silk flowers and plastic pails so the children can put together bouquets. Be sure to include watering cans, sprayers, mini plastic pots, and garden gloves. The children will love pretending they work at the local garden center.

Children at play in the garden center.

Art

- Let the children create dried flower bookmarks. A week or two before this art activity, take small flower heads and leaves and press them between the pages of a large book, such as a dictionary or heavy catalog, and compress them. Meanwhile, cut various colors of heavy oak tag paper into bookmark-sized pieces for each child. Create colored tassels from yarn and set them aside. When you introduce this activity, allow the children to choose the color paper they want. Have them write their names on the back of their bookmark. As a keepsake, date their creation. Show the children the beautiful and delicate flowers you pressed in the book, and let them each choose one. Allow the children to carefully glue and place the spring flowers on the fronts of the bookmarks. After the glue has dried, place clear contact paper over their artwork. Using a hole punch, make a hole in the top of the bookmark and allow the children to pick their favorite tassel to tie through the hole. Send the bookmarks home with the students and encourage the children to read more spring books this season.

Music

- Give children instruments and a microphone. Suggest they create unique songs about the flowers they brought back to the classroom from your spring walk. If you like, tape their singing and title and date the recording. These can be sent home for either a Mother's Day or Father's Day gift, which will be an honored and priceless treasure for years to come.

Closing the First Flowers Theme

Throughout your work with spring's First Flowers activities, ask children questions to increase their comprehension. During your group times, be sure to discuss the purpose of flowers, how pollination occurs, and flowers' importance. Here are some additional questions you can use during activities and to bring this theme to a close:

Why are flowers important?
Why do they have certain smells?
What else do we know about flowers?

Spring Theme 3: Oviparous Animals

Exploring Outside

Take a walk to look for oviparous animals. Oviparous animals develop in an egg and hatch outside their mother's body. Prior to your hike, show children pictures of birds, snakes, fish, turtles, insects, and lizards, to name a few oviparous animals. Point out that bird nests will probably be easiest to spot in spring because many deciduous trees lost their leaves in the fall and only young buds are on the trees now, leaving bird nests exposed. Tell children they can also look for nests of other types of oviparous creatures, such as bees or spiders.

If you are able to spot a nest, ask open-ended questions about it. Questions that point out nests' characteristics and that develop children's language skills might include these:

Why do you think many birds build nests in trees?
Where else would a safe place be to build a nest?
How are nests like our homes?
How many eggs fit in a nest?
What else do you notice?

While you're focusing on nests, be sure to refer to the Winter's Groundhogs, Shadows, and Burrows theme (page 100) and discuss the topic of shelter.

Role Play Outside

While outdoors, explain to the children that they get to curl up and pretend to be animals inside of their eggs. Ask them to coil up tiny and to say the kind of animal they are. Begin by saying, "Let me see what you look like inside your egg." While they pretend to be oviparous babies in their eggshells, children should use "I" statements when answering your questions.

Ask open-ended questions to help them to get into their roles and to develop their higher-level thinking skills:

What does it feel like inside the egg?

What do you think will be the first thing you'll see once you hatch?

What are you looking forward to?

What is happening to you?

Involving Families: Studying Oviparous Animals at Home

Supply the children with some fun activities to do at home. Mention the activities in your weekly newsletter to families. Explain to families that the optional activities are provided for extra quality time together in nature and to involve them in their children's education. Explain that the children are learning about oviparous animals. Remind parents that *oviparous* refers to animals that produce eggs and develop and hatch outside the mother's body. Describe the following nature activities for the families to enjoy at home:

- Ask families to go on a nature hike to observe characteristics of animals that lay eggs.

- Ask parents to discuss with their children the importance of showing respect to all animals.

- Invite families to buy eggs from a grocery store, explain to the children that these are typically sterilized chicken eggs, and cook a favorite egg recipe. They can discuss the food chain and eating relationships between species.

Integrating Nature: Studying Oviparous Animals in the Classroom

Your oviparous animal theme is an egg-cellent topic for curious young minds. Included here are egg-related projects for science, math, writing, art, and other areas. Children will be amazed by all the life forms that develop outside of mothers' bodies. Hatch open these new life activities to get your children exploring this spring.

Science and Discovery

- Allow a small group of children at a time to continue their oviparous animal study. On a tray, provide magnifying glasses and natural items related to oviparous animals. These can include shredded snake skins, old bees' nests, empty birds' nests, and broken eggshells. I have collected these things over my years of teaching, but if they are not at your fingertips, touch base with a science teacher, e-mail your colleagues, or include a request in your weekly family newsletter. Allow children to freely explore these objects. When they've finished, encourage them to draw pictures and write descriptions of what they observed. Younger children can dictate their words for you to write.

- Gather up to ten plastic eggs and different weights. In each egg, insert a weight. If you do not have weights, use coins. Be sure all the weights are different. Number the eggs 1 through 10. Include a scale for children to use in comparing the weighted eggs. Ask them questions, such as, "Which one is heaviest? Which one is lightest?" Having children compare and contrast the differently weighted but same-sized eggs helps them learn about mass, bulk, and solidity.

Math

- Cut out different sizes of ovals the shape of an egg from heavy construction paper. On one side of the ovals, include pictures of oviparous animals. (Use pictures from catalogs or magazines, or draw simple images.) Using one-to-one correspondence, have the children count how many oviparous animals are on the front of each oval. On the backs, write the answers.

  For instance, on the front of one oval, show three snakes, and on the back, write the numeral 3, write the word *three*, and draw three dots, as shown here.

Samantha weighs the plastic eggs that hold mystery weights inside. Austin observes the various oviparous items at the discovery center.

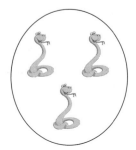
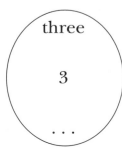

For older children, the ovals could involve addition and look like this:

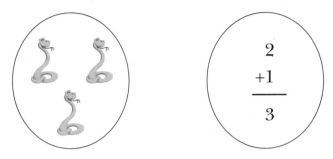

If you create multiple sets of ovals, the game could become a concentration or matching game.

Blocks and Building

- Teach children the concepts *high* and *low* in your blocks and building center. Include many types of plastic oviparous animal toys: turtles, lizards, birds, insects (flying and crawling), and snakes. Next, create a banner titled, "Up high, down low. Where will the oviparous animals go?" Have the children build structures using the blocks. As they place the oviparous animals in, on, and around the structures, encourage them to think about and ask, "Where will the oviparous animals go, high or low?" Children will have to predict whether the particular oviparous animals they are positioning stay low to the ground or are able to fly or climb high. Ask them to say why they put each oviparous animal where they did.

Language Arts

- Have the large group create a predictable book titled *A _____ Is an Oviparous Animal.* Print out a page with the title and make multiple copies for your students. Have each child name his favorite oviparous animal and write (or dictate to you) the animal's name on the blank line. Below their sentence, they will draw their animal and then sign their artwork.

  Allow older children to phonetically spell out the entire sentence on blank pages. The children can indicate their favorite animals to you and copy your written sample of the word, such as *snake,* onto the blank line.

  Later gather and bind all the sheets into a predictable big book you can keep in the writing center. The children will enjoy reading their creations.

Reading

- Provide oviparous animal books for children to explore. Nonfiction books will depict the oviparous animals' natural attributes. Fiction books that include oviparous animals will be enjoyable as well. Some books you can feature include *Chickens Aren't the Only Ones* by Ruth Heller and *Rechenka's Eggs* by Patricia Polacco.

- Include the language arts activity's *A _____ Is an Oviparous Animal.* predictable book in the reading center for children to revisit when they wish.

Writing

- Include sentence strips about oviparous animals. Be sure to make the strips predictable. Repetition helps children develop their early reading skills. Each sentence strip should name a different oviparous animal.

For instance, one strip might read, "A fish hatches from an egg." Be sure to include a picture of a fish next to the word *fish*. Also insert a picture of an egg at the end of the sentence. Including pictures for children with emergent reading skills allows them to feel successful as readers. The next sentence strip may read, "A bird hatches from an egg." Again, include a bird's picture after the word *bird*.

Create many of these strips so the children can view and copy these sentences. Highlight the word *egg* in a different color for easy recognition. Highlight the oviparous animal's name in another color to increase children's awareness and vocabulary. Here are some more example strips:

A child dictates from the sentence strips in the writing center and shows it when she is done.

A fish hatches from an egg.
A bird hatches from an egg.
A snake hatches from an egg.
A lizard hatches from an egg.

Allow the children to independently write and create at this literacy station.

Dramatic Play

- Turn your dramatic play center into a pet store. Create a simple sorting and classifying section by labeling two areas in the dramatic play center: "Oviparous Animal Corner" and "Other Animals Section." Include many stuffed toy animals in these two areas. Bring in identifiable oviparous stuffed play animals, such as ducks, lizards, frogs, snakes, and various birds. For the Other Animals area, provide stuffed play animals of cats, dogs, monkeys, and rabbits. Also supply items the children would need for the pets, such as water dishes, beds, and grooming brushes. The children will enjoy sorting and classifying pets based on their newfound vocabulary word, *oviparous.*

Art

- Model for children the art of egg decorating. Books from the library about egg decorating will be helpful. Slavic styles of egg decorating include Polish *pisanka* egg decorating, Ukrainian *pysanka*, Czech *kraslice*, and Croatian *pisanica* decorating. Mexican decorated eggs, called *cascarones,* are made by hollowing eggs and filling them with confetti. For a true artistic Polish *pisanka* egg, draw with wax on a hard-boiled egg. Then submerge the egg into a dye.

- As an alternative method of teaching children about art made with resists, have them cut out oval shapes that have been copied onto heavy white construction paper or, better yet, heavy white watercolor paper. Explain to the children that they will be making resists. Model and explain how crayons are made from wax. Have the children use crayons to draw designs on their cutout oval papers. Provide watercolors so the children can creatively paint over their wax designs. The design shows up because the drawing is made from wax, which repels, or *resists,* the water. Children will be amazed by their scientific and artistic creations.

Music

- Here are some lyrics you can sing about oviparous animals. Sing "Are You Ready to Hatch?" to the tune of "Frère Jacques":

> **Are You Ready to Hatch?**
> Are you ready to hatch,
> Are you ready to hatch,
> Little duckling, little duckling?
> Will you crack open soon,
> Will you crack open soon,
> Little duckling, little duckling?

> Continue by replacing *little duckling* with *little lizard, ostrich, turtle, snake, fish, ladybug, bee, insect,* or other oviparous animal name. Be sure to vary the animal each time to supply children with many kinds of oviparous animals. After singing this song again and again, children are bound to know which animals hatch from eggs.

Closing the Oviparous Animals Theme

Throughout your work with the Oviparous Animals activities, ask children questions to increase their comprehension. During your group times, be sure to discuss what sets oviparous animals apart from other animals. Here are some additional questions you can use during activities and to bring this theme to a close:

> What happens after an egg hatches?
> How do the animals develop?
> In what ways do all mothers protect their babies?

Spring Theme 4: Miraculous Seeds

Exploring Outside

After reading and reviewing nonfiction books about seeds becoming plants, explain to the children that the class will go on a walk to find a variety of seeds. Pick a day when many dandelions have fully gone to seed. Children are always excited about dandelions' white, fluffy, floating seeds—especially if you suggest they include a wish with the puff of air they use to blow the dandelion apart. Look for a hedgerow, field, or grove of trees where you are most likely to find an assortment of seeds, such as dandelion, maple, oak, and berries. After finding an assortment, encourage the children to study the variations among seeds. Show children the natural selection of seeds in nature.

Ask open-ended questions to encourage the children to examine seeds more closely:

How do you think these seeds got here?
What will happen to them when it rains?
What are your thoughts about the seeds?
What else do you notice?

These are fine questions for your beginning dialogue on miraculous seeds. If you choose to add magical wishes to sending the seed heads aloft, be sure to ask the children questions about their hopes too. They always enjoy sharing their wishes.

Role Play Outside

While outdoors, explain to the children that they get to role-play the seed they find most interesting. Have the children become the seeds, and demonstrate how the seeds travel. Some children may use their arms to fly if they choose a maple's flying helicopter seed. Others may float like the fluffy white parachute of a dandelion flower. Children who chose to depict heavier seeds, such as those of berries, may have to pretend to be carried by a bird and then fall to the ground as part of their travel. Help the children investigate their seed's travel through their role-playing experience.

Remind children to use "I" statements when describing what they're doing as seeds. Tell them that on the count of three, you will be the wind and they will be the seeds. Ask open-ended questions to help the children get into their roles and develop their higher-level thinking skills:

What does it feel like to float on the wind?
Where are you going?
How will you know when it is time to land?
What will happen to you once you land on the ground?

Involving Families: Studying Seeds at Home

Supply the children with some fun activities to do at home. Mention the activities in your weekly newsletter to families. Explain to families that the optional activities are provided for extra quality time together in nature and to involve them in their children's education. Explain that the children are learning about miraculous seeds. Describe the following nature activities for the families to enjoy at home:

- Ask families to go on a nature hike together to find different types of seeds.
- Ask families to discuss with their children how plants help us be healthy. Remind parents to explain that the food we eat, such as beans, corn, lettuce, and tomatoes, helps us to grow strong.
- Remind families to emphasize that their children should never eat unfamiliar plants or ones they can't identify. Tell them to stress that children should always check with an adult before eating any plant.
- Ask families to send in a few seed samples in a ziplock bag. These can be placed in the science and discovery center seed bin or set aside and labeled for further examination and discovery.

Integrating Nature: Studying Seeds in the Classroom

Children enjoy planting seeds and excitedly anticipate their germination. In spring, children enjoy unearthing new life growing under leaf debris.

As an adult, I am still intrigued by seeds. But many people, as they grow from children to adults and become busy with necessary, everyday events, take for granted the miraculous fact that a dried-up, inconsequential-looking seed can produce an abundance of produce. Children appreciate this extraordinary transformation. The following activities help you incorporate the wondrous development of seeds in the areas of science and discovery, math, blocks and building, language arts, reading, writing, dramatic play, art, and music.

Science and Discovery

- In a large bin, provide dehydrated seeds for the children to get their hands in. Dried seeds, such as great northern beans, corn, kidney beans, sunflower, pumpkin, and other varieties will offer a good quality assortment. Allow the children to freely explore in the bin.

- Near the seed bin, add sorting cups and Styrofoam food containers with three or four compartments. Allow the children to sort and classify the seeds by their attributes.

Math

- After getting their hands in seeds at the discovery center, help the children plant a garden at the math center. Prior to introducing your math station, design an 8½ x 11 inch "Plant a Garden" page on your computer. Be sure to include "Gardener's Name" with a blank space for the child's name at the top of the page and include the title "Plant a Garden" below. Allow the children to choose five different types of seeds and to count out five seeds of each type, for a total of 25 seeds. On the "Plant a Garden" page, children can create a garden by gluing five seeds in each of 5 rows. Here is an example:

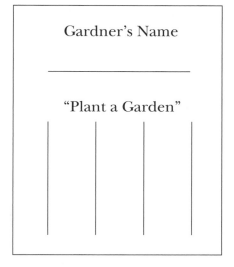

Gardner's Name

_____

"Plant a Garden"

Provide a tub of dried seeds and compartmental plates for the children to sort, classify, and group—a wonderful activity for tactile learners.

Afterward, children can count the seeds using one-to-one correspondence, and then practice counting by fives.

- The Art activity (page 153), which uses seeds to make a labyrinth, or maze, can be integrated into a math lesson by making the labyrinth from *patterns* of seeds.

Blocks and Building

- Children can create raised, rectangular flower beds from blocks. Help children focus on the rectangular shape of each bed. Provide silk flowers and gardening gloves, and supply packing peanuts in a large tub to serve as soil. Include empty flower seed packets for the children to use in their make-believe. They can pretend to pour the seeds and cover them with soil in their beautifully designed rectangular flower beds.

Language Arts

- In the large group, create a predictable book titled *Watch the Seed Grow into a Plant*. Create a page that reads, "Watch the seed grow into a ____." Print a copy for each child. Ask them to name a seed and what type of plant it grows into. The children can write their plants' names in the blank line on the pages. Below the sentence, they can draw a seed-to-plant picture and then sign their artwork.

Provide older children with blank paper and allow them to phonetically spell out the entire sentence. Younger children can indicate their chosen plant to you and copy your written sample of the word, such as *pumpkin* or *nasturtium flower*, on the blank line. When all of the children have finished, gather their pages and bind them into a predictable book. The children will enjoy reading their fine writing and viewing their beautiful illustrations again and again.

Reading

- Provide seed-to-plant books for children to explore. Nonfiction books that depict pollination and other natural attributes of plants are a must. Classic folktales, such as "Jack and the Beanstalk" and stories about other gigantic plants will be fun for the children's imaginations. Some books you can feature include *The Carrot Seed* by Ruth Krauss and *From Seed to Plant* by Gail Gibbons.

Writing

- Include seed-to-plant sentence strips in the writing center. Be sure to make the strips predictable to help children develop strong emergent reading skills. Have each sentence strip include a different seed to plant. For instance, a strip might read, "A bean seed becomes a bean plant," or "A tomato seed becomes a tomato plant." Be sure to include a picture of the plant near the corresponding word. Including such pictures allows children with early reading skills to feel successful about their reading ability.

  Create many of these strips so the children can view and copy the sentences. Highlight the words *seed* and *plant* in different colors to aid word recognition. Here are some sample sentences:

  A bean seed becomes a bean plant.
  A corn seed becomes a corn plant.
  A tomato seed becomes a tomato plant.

  Allow the children to independently write and create at this literacy station.

Dramatic Play

- Reproduce the garden center from the spring First Flowers theme (page 139). Be sure to include play shovels, hoes, and an abundance of silk flowers and plastic pails for them to make bouquets. Offer watering cans, sprayers, mini plastic pots, gardening gloves, and sample flower seed packets, empty or not. From looking at the packets, children will be able to see that the seeds grow into flowers.

  Children will love pretending that they work at the local garden center. As they play, ask them questions about the seeds—for instance, "What kind of flower did that seed grow into?"

Art

- At a sand tray or table, allow the children to create a labyrinth of seeds. Paths that start at the center and move outward are good for teaching labyrinth structure to youngsters. Model this structure, using a variety of seeds.

  If you choose to connect this art lesson to the math activity (pages 150–51), make a labyrinth using a *pattern* of the seeds. Labyrinths have long been used for focus and creativity. They provide a meditative quality for youngsters and adults.

Music

- Use these lyrics to help the children create a song to go with the language arts activity's predictable book, *Watch the Seed Grow into a Plant,* on pages 151–52. Sing "Watch the Seed Grow into a Plant" to the tune of "London Bridge Is Falling Down":

  Watch the Seed Grow into a Plant
  Watch the seed grow into a plant,
      into a plant, into a plant.
  Watch the seed grow into a plant.
  Seeds are miraculous!

  In the next verse, insert *pumpkin, bean, corn, tomato, carrot, flower,* or the name of any other plant in the first line's blank space.

Watch the seed grow into a pumpkin,
into a pumpkin, into a pumpkin.
Watch the seed grow into a pumpkin
Seeds are miraculous!

If you use chart paper to write out your new lyrics, add pictures below the plant names to help young children with their emergent reading skills. Besides teaching plant names, the song teaches children that each seed grows into only one kind of plant.

Closing the Miraculous Seeds Theme

Throughout your work with the Miraculous Seeds activities, ask children questions to increase their comprehension. During your group times, be sure to discuss what seeds need to grow to their full potential. Here are some additional questions you can use during activities and to bring this theme to a close:

What do seeds need to grow?
How do seeds travel?
Why do you think seeds are miraculous?

Spring Theme 5: Tadpoles to Frogs

Exploring Outside

Before heading outdoors, show children the life cycle of a frog. On the Internet or in a nonfiction book about frogs, you are certain to find beautiful pictures of the four life stages of a frog: egg, tadpole, froglet, and adult frog. You have several ways to explore tadpoles outside in the spring. Of course, a favorite outing for all would be to actually visit a nature preserve in your area. If rural or suburban areas surround your school, e-mail your colleagues to ask if anyone has a pond and is willing to offer their natural tadpole resource as a field trip destination for your class. If field trips are out of your school's budget, take a walk near a creek, ditch, conduit, small channel, or even a drainage area where algae tend to form. Any shallow water source will do. You will be likely to find tadpoles if algae are nearby.

When tadpoles are spotted, ask the children some open-ended questions:

Why do you think tadpoles are here?
What do you think they do at night?
What do you think they do during the day?
Do you think they sleep?
Where are their other family members?
What else do you notice?

Role Play Outside

While outdoors, explain to the children that they get to be tadpoles. Ask them to move like tadpoles. Show them how to put their arms behind their backs as straight out as possible and touch their palms together. Suggest they wriggle their arms like the tadpoles' tails. Then have them pretend they are in water. Asking open-ended questions to encourage them to think critically about these future amphibians:

What are you doing?

Where are you going?

What do you like to eat?

What is happening in your home?

Involving Families: Studying Tadpoles and Frogs at Home

Supply the children with some fun activities to do at home. Mention the activities in your weekly newsletter to families. Explain to families that the optional activities are provided for extra quality time together in nature and to involve them in their children's education. Explain that the children are learning about tadpoles and frogs. Describe the following nature activities for the families to enjoy at home:

- Ask families if they have any toy frogs you may borrow during your frog study. The children will be able to snuggle with these cold-blooded vertebrates while reading factual information and fun stories about these amphibious creatures.

- Invite families to take a walk near a body of water and be on the lookout for tadpoles or frogs.

- Suggest families play outside, creating their own unique game of leapfrog. Invite them to write a description of their unique leapfrog game on an index card and send it to school. They can include a picture on the back if they want to. During group time, share these cards with the class. The children will be proud to hear about their families' frog adventures. Next time you head outdoors, bring the cards with you, and the children can practice more leap-froggin' fun.

- Ask families to discuss the importance of frogs with their children; they eat flies and help balance the ecosystem.

Integrating Nature: Studying Tadpoles and Frogs in the Classroom

Be sure to check with your local wildlife agency before collecting tadpoles or eggs. For educational purposes, most will permit a moderate collection of eggs or tadpoles. If you do harvest some, take only a sample for your classroom and leave the remainder where you found them. Choose the largest tadpoles, because they tend to survive best. Bring your bucket of tadpoles back to the classroom for more discovery fun. Children enjoy watching the tadpoles' miraculous development day to day in your science and discovery center. Tadpoles also come into play in math, blocks and building, language arts, reading, writing, dramatic play, art, and music activities.

Science and Discovery

- After your Exploring Outside activity, pour a shallow amount of the tadpoles' water and the tadpoles into a terrarium. Don't use chlorinated tap water, because tadpoles are highly sensitive to it. Be sure to include rocks and algae from the natural water source in the terrarium.

  Provide a simple source for water movement, such as a fountain or aquarium pump, to keep the water oxygenated for the tadpoles. If you are having trouble finding these items to keep tadpoles healthy, ask a science teacher or pet store to set you up with tadpole necessities, ask families for donations from their attic or basement, or buy from a teacher supply catalog.

  Feed some aquarium fish food to the growing tadpoles. A cheaper food is lettuce boiled for ten minutes, finely chopped, and placed sparingly in the water. Leftover lettuce can be kept in the refrigerator.

  Tadpoles will only need a pinch or two of food every week until they have morphed into adult frog bodies, becoming froglets. The time varies, but expect their metamorphosis to occur in ten to twelve weeks. Children will enjoy visiting and observing the daily changes occurring in their tadpole-to-frog terrarium. Be sure to keep your tadpole environment in a shady spot.

- Place a picture chart that depicts the life cycle of a frog in this discovery area. Children can develop their emergent reading and speaking skills by explaining the chart to their friends and helpers in the classroom.

Math

- In your math center, provide plastic toy frogs, pebbles, a small whiteboard, and a marker and eraser for it. If you do not have whiteboard materials, cover a blank piece of heavy construction paper with contact paper and use a whiteboard marker and tissue as an eraser. Write this sentence on the board: "My frog can jump over ____ pebbles." Children will be able to place pebbles at this learning station and count them, using one-to-one correspondence. Afterward, they can demonstrate their number-writing ability by including the numeral on the blank line. See the Writing activity on page 159 for more frog fun. For advanced learners, include many pebbles so children can set up groups of two, five, and ten pebbles. Children can have their frog jump over the sets and practice counting by twos, fives and tens.

Blocks and Building

- Be sure to include in your blocks center some inexpensive plastic frog flip toys, which come in almost every bag of piñata gifts and are available in education catalogs' math-manipulative sections. Encourage the children to build inclines and planes and to keep their frog flipping toy on the slope with each flick. Whether the frogs stay on the slant or not, the children are strengthening both their fine-motor and large-motor skills, and they will love coming up with other frog-flipping fun at this center.

Language Arts

- Create a large picture chart titled "Tadpoles to Frogs." As you and the children progress through the tadpole-to-frog study and read books about frogs and their life cycle, come up with as many facts as possible about the cycle of tadpoles to frogs. As a group, add new facts to the chart and review those you've already written there.

- Make a predictable sentence chart. Use the information you and the children have found to create a large picture chart, "Tadpoles to Frogs." Facts such as these will be helpful:

  Tadpoles begin as eggs.
  Tadpoles swim.
  Tadpoles grow legs.

- Children love to move, so begin a "Hopping Frog Dialogue," providing facts about your baby amphibians. Each child standing in a circle provides a fact about the animals in the Tadpoles to Frogs theme. If a child's fact is true—for example, that tadpoles come from frog eggs—everyone hops once. If a child's fact is not true—for example, that tadpoles don't grow lungs—no one hops until the fact is verified, corrected, and restated as a true fact. For example, the children would change "Tadpoles do not grow lungs" into "Tadpoles grow lungs."

After each fact is offered, ask the class, "Is this a fact or is it not true?" before prompting them to jump or not jump. Children will work diligently to supply factual information so they can continue to hop. This also introduces children to the idea of facts and factual information.

Reading

- Provide nonfiction and fiction books on the topic of frogs for children to explore. Some books you can feature include *An Extraordinary Egg* by Leo Lionni and *Frogs* by Gail Gibbons.

- In the center, place the stuffed frog animals that families have provided so that children can snuggle with and share them while they read about these amphibian creatures.

Writing

- Include sentence strips that begin with "A frog ____." In the blank space, put some Velcro strips—two or three would be best for building sentence structures. Place word cards with Velcro strips on their backs in a bin. Include such phrases as "eats flies," and "hops quickly." If possible, print out pictures to paste next to these words on the cards to aid your early readers. Using the sentence strip and word cards, children can mix and match words as they combine their sentences creatively. This exercise is particularly fun where children deliberately build nonsensical sentences that they can laugh at—all of which is perfect for your goal of having children understand how to build sentences accurately.

- See the math activity on pages 157–58 for more frog fun that incorporates a sentence and writing skills.

Dramatic Play

- *Over* and *under* are wonderful concepts to learn in early childhood. Make learning them fun by playing Hop or Limbo. Using a dowel or broom handle, allow the children to safely practice their large motor skills. To play, have two children each hold one end of the dowel. The others will need to discern by the height of the dowel if they should hop over or limbo under. Continue until everyone has had a chance to participate. Be sure to discuss the safety issues with children when playing this game, such as not raising or lowering the dowel while other children are hopping over or going under. Another variation is to begin by holding the dowel very high and then continuing to lower it until the participant chooses to hop over.

Art

- Have each child cut out one large green oval. This will represent the head and body of the frog. Include white circles for eyes and black markers for creating personality-plus pupils for the eyes. The circles should be glued on the head/body. Next, include four thin green strips for the front and back legs. Children can accordion-fold these to create expandable legs and arms. Glue these to their frog's head and body. Afterward, children can trace their own hands and cut these out for the frog's hands and feet, which are glued to the end of each accordion limb. Finish off with your black marker, and draw one gigantic smile across the oval. You will be amazed at how each child's artistic frog has its own individuality, just as each child has her own uniqueness.

Music

- Use this song to help the children learn concepts like *slow, fast, low, high, far,* and *wide.* Sing "Frogs Can Hop" to the tune of "Row, Row, Row Your Boat":

    Frogs Can Hop
    Frogs can hop so slow.
    This is what they do:
    They hop slow, hop slow.
    You can do it too.

    At the last line, invite children to begin hopping slowly.
    Sing the song again, this time changing *slow* to *fast.* Continue with other concepts, such as *high, low,* and *front to back.*

Closing the Tadpoles to Frogs Theme

Throughout your work with the Tadpoles to Frogs activities, ask children questions to increase their comprehension. During your group times, be sure to discuss interesting facts they've learned about the tadpoles and frogs they've studied. Here are some additional questions you can use during activities and to bring this theme to a close:

What do you like best about these amphibians?
What do you find interesting about metamorphosis?

Spring Theme 6:
Dandy Dandelions

Exploring Outside

In the heart of spring, take the children to your center's play yard, a nearby ball field, or any open area where dandelions are abundant. Notice everything about these plants: the leaves, the flowers, the white fluff of flyaway seeds. Children use their sense of smell, so they will undoubtedly become aware that the blossoming flower heads turn their little noses—and anything else they touch—yellow. Show children the various stages of a dandelion's life. First, show the leaves and explain that some people eat these like lettuce. Second, present a closed dandelion flower, and third, the open yellow dandelion flower. Finally, try to locate a full, white parachute-like dandelion head ready to disperse its seeds. Of course, the empty-seeded stem is another sample to introduce.

Ask open-ended questions throughout your observation, including some about the plant's growth or life stages:

What do you think about the dandelions?
What is the dandelion doing?
Where do the seeds go?
What do you like about these dandelions?
What else do you notice?

The number one spring flower—weed!—picked by children is the dandelion. Children love to observe and pick dandelions and blow dandelion seeds to the wind.

Role Play Outside

While outdoors, explain to the children that they can pretend to be dandelions. First ask them to be the leaves only. Then ask them to grow stems and blossoms. Then have them become the flyaway seeds and finally the empty, seedless stems.

During role play, say, "Let me see what you look like," or ask, "What stage of growth is your dandelion in? Are you the leaf stage only? Are you open, bright, and yellow? Are you closed? Or are you white fluff?" This helps children to take on their roles more fully. Remind children to use "I" statements when they are describing the dandelions they are pretending to be, such as "I am a floating white fluffy dandelion seed!" or "I am a bright yellow dandelion."

Open-ended questions like these help children to develop critical-thinking skills:

What do you look like?
What do you like about yourself?
What is happening to you?

Involving Families: Studying Dandelions at Home

Supply the children with some fun activities to do at home. Mention the activities in your weekly newsletter to families. Explain to families that the optional activities are provided for extra quality time together in nature and to involve them in their children's education. Explain that the children are learning about dandelions. Describe the following nature activities for the families to enjoy at home:

- Ask families to send ten tall dandelion flowers—stem, leaves, and all—in a ziplock bag to school with their child. Be sure to add that they should send in only dandelion flowers that have grown on their own lawn and have not been treated with pesticides or other chemicals. Explain that the children will be looking at the leaves in your discovery center; they will not be eating these samples.
- Use the dandelion stems and flowers for your other integrative activities in the classroom as well.
- Ask families to discuss not eating plants from nature unless an adult has given the okay.
- Ask families to pick full, seeded dandelion heads and blow them to the air as they make wishes. Ask them to record their wishes on index cards and send them into school. Explain that during circle times, you'll read one or two wishes from the children's families to help develop each child's speaking and listening skills.

Teacher Reminder:
Be sure to caution children never to eat anything from nature without having an adult inspect, wash, and prepare the item first. Remind them that some people use chemicals on lawns to prevent weeds, including dandelions, from growing, and the chemicals could be harmful to them.

Teacher Reminder:
If you are still uneasy about chemicals in today's world, before the children examine the greens, give your leaves a good cold wash with a bit of white vinegar or a vegetable wash from the store. Drain the greens in a colander and lay them out to dry on paper towels.

- Ask families to send in the child's baby picture to include in your dramatic play center, which will be turned into a "You are growing like a weed" measuring area.

Integrating Nature: Studying Dandelions in the Classroom

Ask each child to pick many dandelions to bring back to the classroom. Be sure to ask them to bring the leaves and all. Ask the children to pick long-stemmed dandelions for creating many of these activities back inside.

Science and Discovery

- Place pictures and small posters of dandelions in your science and discovery center for reference during other activities.

- Add a small plastic tub of cold water. Have the children turn dandelion flowers with their stems upside down in their hands and begin to peel the hollow stem as if it were a banana. They should peel the stem into four or five separate strips. After they have peeled the stem, have them place the whole dandelion—flower, stem strips and all—in the tub of cold water. Watch in amazement as the long stem strips begin to curl up tightly. Place them on a tray to dry. They can be used later for creating dandelion Art activities (pages 167–68).

- Encourage children to draw pictures of what they did in the discovery center. They can discuss what happened when they placed their peeled dandelion in the cold water and write (or dictate to you) the descriptions on their drawings.

- Include the dandelion leaves in your science and discovery center with magnifying glasses for a closer look. Remind children just to look this time. They will be tasting a sampling of store-bought greens later.

Math

- Offer different lengths of the dandelion stems from the Exploring Outside nature walk for independent comparing and measuring. Provide the children with measuring tools, such as rulers, pencils, snap-block cubes, and blocks, for comparing the different lengths of stems.

- Ask the children to choose ten dandelion stems and to place them in order from longest to shortest.

Blocks and Building

- As in the dramatic play center's "You are growing like a weed!" activity (page 167), during this theme, the blocks and building center will involve more measuring too. Demonstrate to the children how they can measure a plant's height. Provide child-safe tape measures for investigative measuring. Let the children build tall sculptures (my classroom safety rule allows nothing taller than the children's hip height). Every time a child exclaims she is done with her sculpture, offer to help her measure the structure's height.

  First, ask the child to say more about what she built; doing so strengthens language skills. Second, if you are able to, walk around it to view the sculpture from all angles, which will help children develop perception and appreciation skills. Last, measure its height.

  If you are feeling extra ambitious, take a picture, print it, and record the child's full description and the structure's dimensions. This will be a keeper—the child will proudly display her engineering work on the refrigerator at home.

Language Arts

- Prepare an edible dandelion salad for the children to sample. Collect dandelion leaves from a place you know has not been chemically treated. Wash the leaves, drain them in a colander, and gently lay them to dry on paper towels.

  If you would like to enhance your leafy mixture (or forgo handpicking altogether), add a bag of spring mix greens from your local grocery store; it is likely to include dandelion leaves. If you truly want only dandelion greens, your best bet is to find a health food or grocery store that stocks organic foods.

  Provide a small paper plate for each child. Provide a few different dressings on the side, such as ranch and Italian. Invite the children to sample dandelion leaves. Explain to all of the children, especially any who are hesitant to try a taste, that some people eat dandelion leaves like they eat lettuce and that these leaves are used in restaurant salads worldwide. Dandelion leaves are quite nutritious, containing Vitamins A, C, and K, and are also good sources of calcium and potassium.

Teacher Reminder:
If you are uneasy about chemicals in today's world, give your edible leaves a good cold wash with a bit of white vinegar or a vegetable wash purchased from a store.

Teacher Reminder:
Some poisonous plants' leaves can be mistaken for dandelion leaves. If you have any doubt about your identification skills, your best bet is to purchase a small bag of mixed greens that includes dandelion leaves.

For added fun, set up the tables with tablecloths and pretend you are dining in China, where dandelion leaves are typical greens served for dinner. Teachers can serve a few leaves to each child. Encourage everyone to try at least a "No thank you" bite. For those who do try the leaves and like them, offer more of the nutritious greens. While they sample the dandelion leaves, ask the children to describe what they taste like.

- After the dandelion leaves taste test, create a descriptive word chart about the experience. Title the chart "Dandelion leaves taste ____." Record all of the children's responses, and encourage them to use many expressive words.

- Prepare a page that reads, "Dandelion leaves taste ____." Leave space for children to include their name, record their answer, and draw below it. Print enough copies so each child has at least one. Encourage children to write their chosen word in the blank space and to draw pictures of their description in the space below. Younger children can dictate a word to you and then copy your written example. If the child says, for example, "bitter," write down "bitter" on another piece of paper. Then the child can copy the word onto the blank line and draw herself eating bitter dandelion leaves in the space below. Help the children with other descriptive words, such as *delicious*, *good*, *leafy*, and *crunchy*.

- When all the children have finished their drawings, gather and bind them in a predictable book titled *Dandelion Leaves Taste ____*. Read the entire book and tell the children what wonderful authors and illustrators they've become. Afterward, place the book in the reading center.

Reading

- Provide nonfiction dandelion books that depict the actual weed and its attributes. Ask the librarian to include scientific books that include brilliant pictures of dandelions. Fiction books that depict the weedy flower will pique children's interest as well. Some books you can feature include *Dandelions: Stars in the Grass* by Mia Posada and *The Dandelion Seed* by Joseph P. Anthony.

- Include the language arts activity's *Dandelion Leaves Taste ____* predictable book in the reading center for children to revisit when they wish.

Writing

- Write the word *dandelion* on two separate sentence strips. Keep one of the sentence strips intact, and tape it to the top of the writing center. Cut the second strip into the word *dandelion*'s individual letters. Write on more sentence strips the many other words that can be formed using some of the letters of the word *dandelion*. If possible, include pictures for each word, and tape them beside the dandelion strip. These word strips can include *lion, lead, lid, lad, land, lie, dad, and, I, did,* and *add.* Let the children use the cut-apart letters to puzzle out some of these other shorter words that share letters with the long word *dandelion.* Keep the letters and words at the writing center for children to play with independently.

Dramatic Play

- Turn your dramatic play area into a "You are growing like a weed!" measuring area. Post on a posterboard all of the baby pictures the children brought to school. Hang up a banner that reads, "You are growing like a weed!" Provide child-safe measuring tapes to allow the children to measure one another. Ask them to measure the baby dolls in a nearby play crib as well. Children will be able to consider and assess their growth so far. If you are able to include a full-length mirror, you will have a waiting list for the dramatic play center.

Art

- First, take the stems from your science and discovery experiment and set them aside to dry. While you're waiting, take the children outdoors to collect sticks, flat stones, and small pebbles to create dandelion people. Use the stones for their bodies and heads and the dandelion stem curlicues for the hair. The sticks can be used for arms and legs, and tiny pebbles can make features on their faces. As children finish making a dandelion person, discuss the unique qualities each dandelion person has.

   This is an environmentally friendly art activity that can be created outdoors and left for mother nature's dispersal. In the meantime, days can go by and others will come upon it and smile. If you would like to include this as an integrative indoor activity, simply bring these items back to the classroom and allow the children to modify them daily. No glue or paper is needed. Once your dandelion theme is over, return the items to nature for dispersal.

- Place any semidry curly-stem dandelion flowers you didn't use for the dandelion people off to one side. Pull out green construction paper and place yellow tempera paint in cups. Invite the children to dip the dandelion flowers in the yellow paint and stamp unique dandelion prints onto the green construction paper.

Music

- Play some soothing classical music for the children while they pretend to be floating dandelion seeds. Suggest to the children that they try to float upward into the sky to make wishes come true. Demonstrate gracefully on your tiptoes how they can feel lighter than a feather, how they can pretend to be a single dandelion seed.

Closing the Dandy Dandelions Theme

Throughout your work with the Dandy Dandelions activities, ask children questions to increase their comprehension. During your group times, be sure to discuss what is interesting about dandelions. Here are some additional questions you can use during activities and to bring this theme to a close:

What is great about dandelions?
What do they give us?
Why are dandelions interesting?

Spring Theme 7: Finding Stones

Exploring Outside

Take the children outdoors on a hunt for stones. Be sure to have each child bring a plastic shopping bag to hold all the great finds. Head to the playground, near trees and other patches of dirt. For safety, steer clear of streets and parking lots. Without much time or difficulty, most children are likely to find all sorts and sizes of stones.

Once the children have found them, ask unrestricted questions such as these, particularly to help the children consider their decisions and to point out the stones' characteristics:

Why did you choose that stone?
What do you like about that stone?
What does it feel like?
Where do you think it came from?
What else do you notice about your stone?
If you had to say two important things about this stone, what
    would those two things be?
What else do you notice?

The potential for questions is endless.

Role Play Outside

While outdoors, explain to the children that they get to be rocks and stones. Ask them to sit like their stone; remind them that stones do not make noises. Invite them to rest quietly for a moment, feeling only what it is like to be stone. Ask the children, "What do you look like?" Remind them to use "I" statements, such as "I am smooth and round" or "I am small and pointy" when they are pretending to be stones, answering your questions, or talking about themselves. Taking time to allow the little stones to roll down a hill or perform other movements would be great for your kinetic learners.

Draw out children's descriptive words by asking open-ended questions. Here are some questions you can use, and of course the wonderful question that keeps popping up throughout all your role-playing segments: "What is the best thing about being you?"

How did you get so smooth?
Why are you so rough?
What do you do out here?

Involving Families: Studying Stones at Home

Supply the children with some fun activities to do at home. Mention the activities in your weekly newsletter to families. Explain to families that the optional activities are provided for extra quality time together in nature and to involve them in their children's education. Explain that the children are learning about stones. Describe the following nature activities for the families to enjoy at home:

- Invite family members to go on a stone hunt together to find the perfect stone. Suggest they place it somewhere special in their home and use it as a family message holder. Explain that the families can include paper and pencils next to the stone and encourage the children to draw or write a message on the paper. Messages can be as simple as a smiley face or "I love you!" Adults should feel free to write playful or responsible messages in return. A playful response might be "I love you too!" Responsible messages might include "Remember to wash your hands." All family messages can be placed under the family message holder. The family message holder is simply a way to increase adult communication with children. This fun activity for home offers a gesture toward greater communication within families.

- In concluding your stone exploration, ask families to send in one item for your classroom's stone soup recipe in the Reading activities on page 173. Items can include vegetable broth and canned or fresh vegetables. The children will enjoy being a part of this fine-character cooperative group learning experience.

Integrating Nature: Studying Stones in the Classroom

After your class does the Exploring Outside and Role-Playing Outside exercises, have each child bring an array of stones back to the classroom. They will be able to play in various centers with their newfound natural stones. Since the dawn of humans, people have used stones to help themselves think creatively. The children in your care will be no different.

Science and Discovery

- Be sure to include the following items in your science and discovery center to help the children explore stones: a few magnifying glasses, a small scale, a larger slate or chalkboard, and sorting plates. Allow children to independently sort and classify stones based on the attributes they've chosen. Some might classify and sort by size. Others might do so by color, texture, or another quality. By allowing children to independently explore and classify, you encourage them to use and strengthen their critical-thinking skills.

Math

- Provide the children with a tray of several stones about the same size that can be used as weights. Next, supply a scale and various small items to weigh. Any classroom or office item will do, such as a stapler, tape dispenser, package of markers, or box of crayons. When you have collected the items, take a picture of each and print it. Tape each picture on a whiteboard or laminated piece of paper that reads, "The ____ weighs ____ stones." Move one picture into the first blank. The children will use a dry-erase marker to write their answer on the second, or measurement, blank. For example, after weighing the tape dispenser, they might write "14" in the measurement space of the sentence. Provide children with a tissue for an eraser. They will enjoy using their math skills as they continue to weigh all the objects. This activity gives children practice in using a scale, counting with one-to-one correspondence, and writing their numbers. Guide the children by asking them questions, such as "Which object weighed more, the tape dispenser or the stapler?" Watch in amazement as the children independently come up with ideas at this center.

- Another fine activity involving stones is to create a tic-tac-stone game for two players. Find four long sticks to create a tic-tac-toe board. Next, have each player gather nine stones that look very similar—for example, all gray or of a comparable smoothness. These will be the tic-tac-toe pieces. Each player's stones should be different enough that you can easily identify whose pieces are on the board. Have fun with this favorite traditional pastime.

- The writing center's live graph activity on page 173 is also a good Math connection activity.

Blocks and Building

- Include different sizes of rocks and stones in your blocks and building center. Provide pictures of balancing stones and buildings that include both wood and stone. Allow the children to create their own unique structures using stones and blocks.

- Children can form inclines and planks for stones to move and roll on. To help them take pride in their work, photograph their creations and post them in the center. Tell the children they could grow up to be architects, designers, or engineers. When they are allowed to create in this center, they will develop early problem-solving skills.

- Another option for the blocks and building center is to provide a small pail of stones and some trucks so the children can haul the stones and continue their construction play.

Language Arts

- Pass around two very different types of stones for children to examine. Then create a Venn diagram using the two stones as subjects. A Venn diagram shows that although each stone has its own unique qualities, both share a connection because of other, similar characteristics.

  A Venn diagram includes two circles, one for each stone. The circles intersect. Where the circles overlap or merge in the center, write down the characteristics that both stone 1 and stone 2 share. Where a circle does not overlap, write the characteristics that are unique to one stone only. In the example below, both stones are cool, gray, and white, so those words are in the merged area. Other characteristics that are specific to only one stone stay within that stone's own circle. This exercise also helps children build a repertoire of adjectives.

Stone 1		Stone 2
attractive small bumpy	cool gray white	large smooth round

Reading

- Provide a variety of fiction and nonfiction picture books that offer good pictures and descriptions of rocks and minerals. This will be helpful when the children naturally seek more information on interesting stones. Some books you can feature include *Stone Soup* by Marcia Brown and *If You Find a Rock* by Peggy Christian.

- As a group time activity, read one of the many versions of the classic tale "Stone Soup." Later ask families for help in creating a stone soup recipe in the classroom. (See the Involving Families section, page 170.)

Writing

- Provide a tray of tiny to small stones in your writing center. Laminate an 8½ x 11 inch sheet with the word *stone* printed on it. Model for the children how to use many tiny stones to trace and cover the word *stone*. As the children independently practice writing the word *stone*, praise them and tell them what great spellers they are!

- For a more advanced activity, have the children turn over the laminated paper to its blank side. This time they can practice writing the word *stone* without having the word to trace.

- Also include premade sentence strips that include fun ideas for using a stone. Here are some examples:

  You can skip a stone on water.
  You can draw on the sidewalk with a stone.
  You can make a bug path in the dirt with a stone.

Read each sentence strip to the children. Create a live graph by asking them to stand behind the sentence strip that describes what they would like to do with a stone. For instance, six children might stand behind the "skip a stone" strip, four might be behind the "draw on sidewalk" strip, and two might choose the "bug path" strip. During this activity, discuss graph terms, such as *most, least,* and *more than.* When you ask children higher-level, critical-thinking math questions, such as how many more children are at the skip-a-stone strip than at the bug path strip, children will have to use their higher math abilities for interpreting the live graph. After this group activity, tape the sentence strips at the writing center for the children to independently write and create illustrations.

- After center time, take the tray of stones outdoors for some fun interacting with nature outside. Allow the children to play hopscotch, draw pictures, and make bug paths. If you have standing water, demonstrate how to skip stones and let the children try.

Dramatic Play

- Make your dramatic play center a tranquil stone area for this theme. Borrow a desktop stone fountain. (Or better yet, purchase one for yourself and take it home to enjoy when your stone theme is finished.) Place some small stones near the fountain so the children can balance them off to one side. Nearby, add a few small couch pillows for the children to sit on, and enjoy watching them practice their listening skills. Model how to sit quietly on the pillow, with backs straight. Show them how you gaze at the water in the stone fountain and the balance stones. Demonstrate by thinking aloud, "I love to sit here quietly and listen to the water flowing on the stones. This feels very peaceful."

Art

- Connect your math center's weight lesson to art by creating one-of-a-kind paperweights for the children to take home. Take them outside on a one-of-a-kind stone hunt. Allow each child to pick a larger stone of his own choosing. These will be used for the children's one-of-a-kind paperweights. Back in the classroom, have the children wash their stones. They will need to write their names in permanent marker on the bottom of their stones. For an added treasure, include the date, since these paperweights will likely be valued for years to come.

Meanwhile, prepare cups of tempera paint, providing one paintbrush and one paint color per cup. Allowing the children to choose one of four or five colors for their base coat will add individuality to their paperweights. The children will be very proud of their independence. When they've chosen a color, they can paint their stones' base, being careful to paint only the top of the rock. When the base coat is dry, the children can use smaller paintbrushes to create unique designs using the other colors available. The designs can be as creative as they wish. When the designs are dry, paint or spray the stone with a clear luster or gloss coating for a polished finish. Voilà! Each child has a one-of-a-kind paperweight that can be used at home to hold important papers or to serve as his family's message holder stone.

Stones found outdoors by the children one sunny day and painted in the classroom on a rainy day.

- Look at pictures of labyrinths on the Internet or in library books before heading outdoors to create one. Tell the children they'll be doing an environmental art activity. Explain to them that the beauty of environmental art is that you get to appreciate the process and the moment. By using the term "the moment," you help the children develop an appreciation for the present. Explain that most environmental art dissipates and goes back to the earth.

  Begin the outdoor labyrinth by gathering many stones of different sizes. Sort the stones into three separate piles: small, medium, and large. Next, have the children create paths and swirls for a unique labyrinth. Afterward, talk about the experience of making this creation. Point out that when they were cooperatively working together, things went smoothly. Discuss the word *cooperation*.

Music

- Here's a song to help children keep anxiety at bay. Show children a favorite stone they can carry in their pocket and hold onto when they become worried or scared. Sing "The Worry Stone Song" to the tune of "Bingo." Children love to clap as they spell the word *stone*.

The Worry Stone Song
I hold my stone if I get scared.
It helps me to be worry free.
S-t-o-n-e, s-t-o-n-e, s-t-o-n-e,
And I'll be worry free!
When I'm afraid, I hold my stone.
Let go of fear is the key.
S-t-o-n-e, s-t-o-n-e, s-t-o-n-e,
And I'll be worry free!

Closing the Finding Stones Theme

Throughout your work with the Finding Stones theme, ask the children questions to increase their comprehension. During your group times, be sure to discuss interesting things they've learned about stones. Here are some additional questions you can use during activities and to bring this theme to a close:

How do you think stones are formed?
How are stones helpful to us?
What are some interesting items you have learned about stones?

Summer Nature Study
June, July, August

Summer Reading List

Here is a list of the books I recommend providing the children throughout the summer themes:

Asch, Frank. *The Sun Is My Favorite Star.*
Brinckloe, Julie. *Fireflies!*
Cole, Henry. *On Meadowview Street.*
Cole, Joanna. *The Magic School Bus: Inside a Beehive.*
Cronin, Doreen. *Diary of a Fly.*
Demi. *The Empty Pot.*
Fleming, Denise. *In the Tall, Tall Grass.*
Gibbons, Gail. *From Seed to Plant.*
————. *Sun Up, Sun Down.*
Hoose, Philip M., and Hanna Hoose. *Hey Little Ant.*
Hubbell, Patricia. *Sea, Sand, Me!*
McDermott, Gerald. *Arrow to the Sun; A Pueblo Indian Tale.*
Munsch, Robert. *The Sandcastle Contest.*
Pinczes, Elinor J. *One Hundred Hungry Ants.*
Rustad, Martha E. H. *Honey Bees.*

Basking in Warmth and Abundance

Summer is the season of abundance. Plants are in full bloom, the daylight is rich, and the outdoors can be a favorite hotspot. For the senses, summer is a feast. In this chapter, we consider summer's characteristics and discover the lush abundance of the season. Summer is the transition from spring to fall, the change from moderate to warmer temperatures. The richness of this season focuses on full blooms, brightness, and warmth. It provides us with plenty to enjoy. Growth, heat, and fullness are a few of summertime's treasured characteristics. Appreciation comes to mind as the season blossoms in and around us. Summer is the perfect season to sit back, relax, and reflect on how we want to blossom as educators and help children become radiant as well.

My Summer Reflection

Reflecting back now, I see my fascination with summer had to do with how I occupied my time during the longest days of the year. I brought to the season my relaxed attitude and my desire to closely observe everything under the sun. I spent hours lying on my back daydreaming, watching cumulus clouds form cows and transform into giant castles. Summer was filled with this type of abundance. Swimming, playing in sprinklers, and walking barefoot were my favorite seasonal pastimes.

All before lunchtime, my friend and I would climb trees and carve small pictures with sharp stones in the soft bark, weave leaf crowns, draw with sticks in the dirt, and make mud pies and sculptures. (Perhaps you get an inkling why twenty-five years later I would take up environmental art as an emphasis for my art certification.) After lunch, neighborhood friends played kickball and tag, and when evening approached, the activities turned to hide-and-seek. Once the streetlights came on and I returned home, my mom would roll her eyes at my soiled summer self and point me to the bathtub. There was a comfort in crawling into my clean bed and gazing out my bedroom window at the bright moon and sparkling stars in the big summer sky. The curtains blew in the warm breeze, and I would fall asleep to the chirp of crickets while dreaming about summer's abundance.

Your Summer Reflection

Let us jump right into discovering summer abundance and the warm weeks ahead. What has summer meant to you? Perhaps you grew up in the city, and running through the opened fire hydrants cooled you off. Maybe you played under the shade of an overhanging rock ledge and still felt the simmering sandy heat of the desert. Do you recall flying Frisbees with your family in the park, swimming at the public pool, barbecuing in the backyard, drinking lemonade on the patio, or staying up late to identify the constellations while roasting marshmallows by a bonfire?

What summer memories come to your mind this time of year? A teacher reflection for you to use during this plentiful season follows. As you anticipate each season, use the reflection as a beginning balancing point for your own sense of appreciation of the season in front of you. Remembering the good times outside, whether you are reflecting on these memories while literally outdoors or thinking about your past good times while outside, it is a superb place to take in nature and all the fullness summer has to offer. Reflection is always a helpful balancing source to use when working with little ones. It is a healthy format you can use with all the seasons.

What reminiscent summer stories do you have? Which ones will you share with your students? This is an opportunity for you to bring summer and all its rich life and traditions to the young minds in front of you. Doing so provides the children with appreciation for nature on another level and will entice them to get outdoors and create their own memorable summer stories!

Here are some lists and questions to ponder as the current season enters your spirit and classroom.

What does summer mean to you?

_____

_____

_____

_____

_____

What has this season meant to you in the past?

_____

_____

_____

_____

_____

What past stories come to your mind?

_____

_____

_____

_____

_____

How will you personally take time to enjoy this season?

_____

_____

_____

_____

_____

What are you thankful for this summer season?

_____

_____

_____

_____

_____

How will you set the tone for the season ahead?

_____

_____

_____

_____

_____

Are there any special activities you can include to bring in the season in your own way?

_____

_____

_____

_____

_____

Sing in the Season

Begin the season with a song to say good-bye to the season you have just finished and welcome the season ahead. By continuing to do this with all the seasons, you help children to strengthen their predictive skills. By the end of the year, the children will shout, "Let's sing the good-bye–hello song!" Praise them for their strong memory skills. All of this gives the children a simple ritual for saying good-bye to the season they have just enjoyed. It helps them appreciate the newness of the coming season and welcome it with all of its blossoming surprises. Building that healthy sense of saying good-bye, letting go, and surrendering to what is in front of us is another wonderful skill nature can teach us. Sing "Good-bye, Spring! Hello, Summer!" to the tune of "Good Night, Ladies":

Good-bye, Spring! Hello, Summer!
Good-bye, spring; good-bye, spring; good-bye, spring;
We enjoyed you so!

Hello, summer; hello, summer; hello, summer;
We welcome you right now!

Invite Families to Participate

Bring families on board to notice summer and investigate new life with their children. Send home a brief letter to families to introduce your nature activities for summer. Remember you are helping tremendously by including families in your getting-children-outdoors mission and wholesome environment education. Ask families to provide pictures and summer signs, such as flowers, shells, grass, sand, or anything else that will bring the summer topic to curious young minds. Here is a sample introductory letter to send home:

Dear Families,

Happy almost summer! In preparing for the upcoming summer season in our classroom, we will be asking for your help in the weeks ahead. The children will soon be delving into these summer topics at school:

- Summer's Insects
- Ready for the Sun
- Summer's Grass
- Relaxing with the Sand
- Busy Honeybees
- Picnic Ants
- Bloomin' Flowers

Be on the lookout this summer for our simple nature homework activities. These will all be wholesome, fun family activities that will provide enjoyment for the season, such as looking for insects in nature, getting some vitamin D by reading together in the sunshine, and talking about summer plants and other summer attributes. In the meantime, please send in a simple summer treasure with your child to school. These will be added to our Summer Family Treasures box. Items can include such things as a picture of a fun family summer activity, special shells you found on the beach during a summer vacation, or a flowering plant you and your child planted together. We will be discussing all of these individual items during our group circle time. Our group time discussions will enhance the children's listening, speaking, reading, and writing skills and provide an opportunity to integrate the seasonal theme in all their learning.

Thank you in advance for all of your summer contributions. More important, thank you for your involvement in your child's education! As a side note, you are probably well aware that today's children need more time outdoors enjoying nature. They need time to appreciate the simple things our environment has to offer. I value having you join me in helping with this important task.

Here's to celebrating the summer season and all of its gifts.

My best to you,
[insert your signature here]

Decorate a shoe box or other box with summery construction paper and decorations. Be as creative as you wish. Label the box "Summer Family Treasures." When the children bring their treasure items to school, have them put the items in the summer treasure chest. Later let each child teach about the original items during your group meeting time.

In your weekly newsletters, remind families of any specific requests this season, such as going on an insect walk or tossing a ball around together in the summer sun. In the newsletter, also mention the upcoming optional home activities that are created to help families and their children connect with nature and all its richness.

Summer Theme 1: Summer's Insects

Exploring Outside

Before taking the children outdoors to look for insects, show them a variety of pictures of insects on the Internet or in a nonfiction book. Explain to the children that they will be looking for insects on the playground, in the grass and dirt, and near trees. Remind the children that they are looking for insects—bugs that have a head, thorax (chest), abdomen, and six legs. Bring along magnifying glasses for a closer look.

Once the children have found insects, ask them open-ended questions such as these to think more deeply about their six-legged creatures' characteristics:

What do you think the insects are doing?
Why do you think these insects have wings (or not)?
Do you think they get tired?
I wonder how they communicate with other insects.
How do they eat?
How do they remember where they live?
What else do you notice?

The potential for questions is endless.

Role Play Outside

While outdoors, explain to the children that they get to be insects. Ask them to choose a crawling or a flying one and to move like that insect. Join in the fun and pretend you are a scientist trying to catch insects to inspect. Begin by asking, "What do you look like?" and "What do you sound like?" Remind the children to use "I" statements when they respond while pretending to be the bugs.

Asking open-ended questions gives children a chance to use their language skills and develop their thought processes. Here are some fine open-ended questions you could use:

Why do you have wings (or not)?

What do you do for fun?

What is the best thing about being you?

Are you ever afraid of anything, since you're so small in the world?

Involving Families: Studying Insects at Home

Supply the children with some fun activities to do at home. Mention the activities in your weekly newsletter to families. Explain to families that the optional activities are provided for extra quality time together in nature and to involve them in their children's education. Explain that the children are learning about very small but important creatures: insects. Describe the following nature activities for the families to enjoy at home:

- Ask families to go on a short insect walk with their child. Have them help him identify as many insects as possible. Remind them that insects are creatures with these body parts: head, thorax, abdomen, and six legs. Ask them to send a short list of all the types of insects they viewed on their walk—for example, beetles, flies, bees, dragonflies. When the children bring their lists to school, compare the similarities and differences among the lists.

- Ask families to discuss the importance of insects and why we should never hurt them. For instance, ladybugs eat aphids, which are harmful to plants. Bees make honey. Other insects serve as food for birds.

Integrating Nature: Studying Insects in the Classroom

It would be fine to catch a few insects for the brief amount of time you are Exploring Outside as a class. However, remind the children before going back inside that the insects will be visiting your classroom for only a day or two. Explain that nature's insects belong in nature because the insects know better than we humans what they need to do outdoors, what they need to eat, and how to take care of themselves. Within a day or two, simply release the insects and focus on the importance of leaving nature's insects out

Keefer watches cockroaches climbing, eating, and socializing inside a borrowed classroom terrarium.

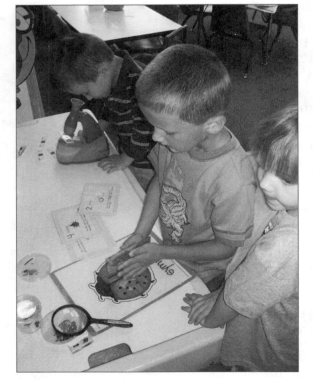

Keefer uses a mirror and a magnifying glass to study the symmetry of a ladybug on a poster.

in nature. The children can wave good-bye to the insects and enjoy plenty of other insect-related activities.

Science and Discovery

- Provide petri dishes of insects that for one reason or another didn't survive in the natural world. Look for insects on windowsills or porches. Instead of throwing them in the garbage or sweeping them back to the earth, lay cotton in the bottom of a small petri dish and place the deceased bug on top. Tape the petri dish closed so the children can look into the dish but not open it. Remind them to be respectful of the dead insects. Tell them they are not to shake the dishes, but they can use magnifying glasses to more closely observe the insect's head, thorax, abdomen, and six legs.

- Include posters of various insects in your science area. Also include a microscope for an even closer look when the children place the petri dishes of real insects under it.

- Include abandoned bees' nests in your science center.

Math

- Provide a bucket of plastic toy insects, bugs, and other creepy crawlies, even including such animals as worms and snakes. Allow the children to explore the toy insects freely.

- Later supply sorting trays and model for the children how to sort insects (with a head, thorax, abdomen, and six legs) from other bugs and creepy crawlies with multiple legs and other characteristics. Including worms, snakes, and various bugs will expand the children's sorting and classifying abilities.

Blocks and Building

- Include letter development in your blocks and building center by modeling for the children how to spell the word *Insects* using curved and straight blocks. Begin by typing the word *Insects* in a simple block font and printing out the page to use as a poster. Glue pictures of insects all around the word and hang the poster in your block area. Next, show the children how to use curved blocks to make curvy letters, such as *c* and *s,* and how to use straight blocks to make straight letters, such as *t* and *I.* Include a bucket of plastic toy insects for the children to place on top of the block word. Ask the children, "What do all those letters spell?" As they independently practice, praise them, saying, "Wow, you spelled the word *Insects* using blocks and toy insects. Great spelling!" Use this block and building idea in your Busy Honeybees (page 215) and Picnic Ants (pages 221–22) themes as well.

The students sort and classify plastic insects.

Language Arts

- As a large group, create a predictable book titled *A _____ Is My Favorite Insect.* Begin by printing a page that includes the sentence "A _____ is my favorite insect." Print or copy one page for each child.

  After reading several books about insects, allow the children to name their favorite insect. Let younger children tell you the insect's name, and then write it on a small, separate sheet of paper so they can copy that word onto their page. For instance, if a child shared that her favorite insect is a butterfly, write the word *butterfly* on a separate piece of paper and ask the child to copy the word into the blank space. Ask older children to try to phonetically spell out the name of their favorite insect in the blank space. Underneath the sentence, the children can draw their favorite insect then sign their work at the bottom of the page.

Regardless of their ages, all children will take pleasure in seeing their illustrations when you've collected and bound the pages together into a book.

- During circle time, read the predictable part of the book as a whole group. Keep the laminated classroom book in the reading center. The children will love to show how they can read and will revel in seeing each other's artwork.

Reading

- Provide insect books in your reading center for children to explore. Nonfiction books that depict actual insects and their body parts will be great for your curious children. Many books include bright pictures and 3-D images. Children will enjoy putting on their 3-D glasses to view the illustrations. Fiction books that play with the behavior of various insects will pique their interests as well. Some books you can feature include *Fireflies!* by Julie Brinckloe and *Diary of a Fly* by Doreen Cronin.

- Include the language arts activity's *A _____ Is My Favorite Insect* predictable book in the reading center for children to revisit when they wish.

Writing

- Provide sentence strips that include sentences containing the word *insect* and describing the type of insect. This gives children the time to practice and review sight words, such as *a, is,* and *an.* Children will be able to view and copy these strips in the writing center. To encourage early word recognition and one-to-one reading correspondence, use a different-colored marker to write the word *insect.* For more correspondence reading, use other colored markers for the actual insect words, such as *butterfly, ladybug, bee,* and *beetle.* Including pictures on the strips helps children's early reading skills. Here are some sample strips to include:

    A butterfly is an insect.
    A ladybug is an insect.
    A bee is an insect.
    A beetle is an insect.

    Allow the children to write and create independently at this literacy station.

Dramatic Play

- Turn your dramatic play center into a summertime nature center. If you have a tree or plant and some real flowers, perfect! Just place them around your center, making the greenery as lush and abundant as possible to get the full summer effect. Otherwise, silk flowers and an artificial tree will do, or homemade flowers and a painted cardboard tree—either can make this area look summery.

  Next, make necklaces to hang in the area from pictures of various insects. Be sure to include an equal number of flying and crawling insects. (You could include honeybees and ants, too, since we will revisit this play area with our upcoming summer themes of Busy Honeybees and Picnic Ants.) Glue each picture separately on a circular piece of construction paper. Write with a marker, "I am a flying insect," or "I am a crawling insect." Highlight the words *flying* and *crawling*. Laminate the pictures, and punch a hole and thread yarn for a necklace. Children can choose if they want to be a crawler or flyer by wearing the corresponding necklace. They can pretend to be a flying or crawling insect around the nature center.

  To increase their inquiry and critical thinking, ask children open-ended questions:

  > Why did you choose to be the beetle [or whichever insect necklace they are wearing]?
  > What do you like best about being a beetle?
  > What do you like best about being a flying [or crawling] insect?

  Children will enjoy returning to this area again and again, especially during the upcoming Busy Honeybee and Picnic Ant summer themes.

Art

- A simple art activity can be done using symmetry to create abstract, artistic ladybugs. Copy a large circle onto 8½ x 11 inch red construction paper. Have the children cut out the circles and then fold their papers in half. Open up the circular paper as if it were a greeting card. Using small paintbrushes and black tempera paint, children can place five tiny black dots of paint on one side of the paper only. Count the dots together. Then fold the paper in half and smooth the sides together. Unfold it and ask the children to count the dots again. Provide black paper, glue sticks, and white crayons for children to add six legs, a head, thorax, and antennas.

- As a science and math bonus, provide mirrors at the art center for the ladybug creations. After children open their creations, model for them how to place a mirror in the center of their art work and view their symmetrical designs this way. Remove the mirror so they can view their actual artwork. Ask the children to define *symmetry*, and discuss the word with them.

Music

- Write the lyrics to "An Insect" on a chart paper. Add pictures for the words *insect, head, thorax, abdomen,* and *legs* to help in one-to-one word reading correspondence. After reviewing the lyrics on the chart with the children, sing "An Insect" to the tune of "Row, Row, Row Your Boat":

  An Insect
  An insect has three parts
  To its buggy body:
  Head, thorax, abdomen.
  Its six legs help it move.

Closing the Summer's Insects Theme

Throughout your work with Summer's Insects, ask children questions to increase their comprehension. In your group times, be sure to discuss why insects are important. Here are some additional questions you can use during activities and to bring this theme to a close:

Why are insects important?
What do insects give us?
How do insects help us and other animals?

Summer Theme 2: Ready for the Sun

Exploring Outside

Watch the weather and select a sunny day for learning about the sun's warmth. Send home a brief note a few days beforehand asking families to apply sunscreen to their children for your sun-filled fun day. Ask them also to send along sun hats, sunglasses, and beach towels for your sunny exploration.

Before going outside, explain to the children why they have sunscreen on today. Show them a bottle of SPF 30 sunscreen, and explain the importance of sunscreen for protecting them from harmful ultraviolet A and ultraviolet B rays. Also talk about vitamin D, which the sun creates in their bodies, and the importance of getting outside in sunshine daily.

Then invite the children to take their beach towels outside for some fun in the sun. Once outside, lay out the beach towels and have the children lie on them, close their eyes, and feel the sun's warmth.

Ask the children open-ended questions to help them develop strong communication skills:

How does it feel to relax in the sun?
What does the sun feel like on your face?
What else do you notice in the sky?
Pretend to be at the beach—what is it like?
Pretend to be in the desert—what is it like?
What else do you notice?

Role Play Outside

While outdoors, explain to the children that you are going to choose one of them at a time to be the sun. While the others continue to sit or lie on their towels, have one child stand up to be the sun. Tell her to circle her hands and arms around her head to be the large sun that warms the earth and all of the people and animals. Keeping her circled arms above the other children, have the sun pretend to shine and warm the others on their beach towels. Take turns choosing other children to be the sun. Ask the sun open-ended questions like these:

What are you doing?
What does it feels like to warm everything on earth?

Afterward, allow the children to play outside in the sun.

One fun game to play is Don't Get Sunburned, a version of tag. Show the children the area in which everyone will play. You can indicate a playground area or cone off a small section of the school grounds. This game is played in five- to seven-minute segments. Begin by choosing a child to be the sun. Next, show the children where the designated "You Are Out—Cooling Off in the Shade" area will be. If a child is tagged, this is where she sits out.

Start the game by calling, "Don't get sunburned!" Encourage all the children to run from the sun. If the child who is the sun tags another child, the tagged child has to sit out in the cooling-off area. A child is safe and cannot be tagged if she is in a shaded area other than the cooling-off one. After five to seven minutes, choose another child to be the sun. To end the game, the sun who tagged the most children sitting in the cooling-off area wins.

To play a shorter version of this game, the teacher becomes the sun and tries to tag the children. Remember, children truly do not care who wins in a tag game. They simply enjoy the chasing and frolicking in nature.

Involving Families: Studying the Sun at Home

Supply the children with some fun activities to do at home. Mention the activities in your weekly newsletter to families. Explain to families that the optional activities are provided for extra quality time together in nature and to involve them in their children's education. Explain that the children are learning about our solar system's star, the sun. Describe the following nature activities for the families to enjoy at home:

• For your Exploring Outside segment, remind the adults to apply sunscreen to their children for their sun-filled activities. Suggest they also discuss the importance of sunscreen and how to avoid getting sunburned.

- Ask families to include a little vitamin D time in their daily schedule by going outside together and tossing a ball around or throwing a Frisbee to one another. Or for relaxation and vitamin D, read a book together while sitting outside in the sunlight; remind them to wear UV protection over their eyes when they do. Emphasize that children should be getting ample amounts of vitamin D by getting outside in the sun for several minutes each day.

- Ask adults in the family to share with their child what their favorite sun-filled activity was when they were young.

Integrating Nature: Studying the Sun in the Classroom

When we think of the sun, we immediately think of warmth and light. Included in these next integrative activities, you will find not only warm temperatures and light but some cool ways for staying cool in the heat and for learning more about the sun.

Science and Discovery

- Set up your science and discovery center with pictures of the sun. Include outer space pictures, sun rising and setting pictures, and pictures of people having fun in the summer sun—for example, people by the pool drinking iced tea or lemonade, or having fun in the water. Such pictures and photographs help children identify attributes of the summer season and teach them the basics about summer weather and dressing for the season.

    Also provide three cups and three thermometers. In cup number one, pour moderately warm water; in cup number two, pour room temperature water; in cup number three, pour refrigerated ice water. Allow the children to use their fingers to feel the temperature of each water cup and then to place the thermometers in each cup. Help them to read the temperature of each water cup. For instance, cup one might read 81 degrees, cup number two might read 67 degrees, and cup number three might read 42 degrees. Ask the children questions to encourage critical thinking:

    Which cup would be best for drinking water? Why?
    Which one would be best for taking a bath in? Why?
    Which one do you think would be most fun to swim in?

    Be sure to have the children explain their answers. Doing so strengthens their newfound knowledge.

Math

- Include manipulative items of these colors in your math center: yellow (for the sun), blue (for the sky), and white (for clouds). The items can be shape blocks, snap-block cubes, or any other item your kinetic and tactile learners will enjoy handling and working with. Put all the items on a tray. Model for the children different sorting techniques. Think aloud as you sort. Certainly sorting by color attributes is a simple technique that all children can feel successful at. Say, "I'm going to sort all the yellow ones first—yellow like the sun." Then begin by taking the yellow items off the tray and placing them to one side. Do this with all the colors. Also show them how to arrange by size and shape. The children are certain to come up with other sorting attributes as well.

  Illustrate different ways to create patterns. For instance, show the children yellow = a, blue = b, and white = c. Then begin an A-B pattern by pulling a yellow item, then a blue item, then a yellow item, then a blue item. Model an A-B-C pattern and an A-BB-C pattern as well. Ask the children to show you what patterns they have made. They will enjoy showing you patterns they have created on their own. Allow the children to independently create, sort, and pattern in this math center.

Blocks and Building

- To cool off during this sunny study theme, have the children engineer different sizes and shapes of swimming pools. Include in your blocks center pictures of swimming pools of different sizes and shapes. The children will enjoy using their blocks to make kidney-shaped, rectangular, circular, and oval pools. For more fun in the sun, include extra sunglasses and some pool toys for the children to play with after their invented swimming pool shape is created.

Language Arts

- Prior to this activity, create on a blank 8½ x 11 inch page a sentence that reads, "I like to _____ in the sun." Be sure to include space for a child's name and a drawing. Print enough copies so each child can have at least one.

Next, create a classroom picture chart titled "I like to _____ in the sun." During large-group time, ask each child to share one thing he likes to do in the sun. Record the children's responses next to their names on the chart.

- Later give children the "I like to _____ in the sun" pages. You can write younger children's dictated responses on the blank line. Somewhat more advanced learners can copy their response from the class chart. Older children who are ready can phonetically spell out their response on the blank line. Allow the children to independently illustrate their response on their pages.

- Collect all the children's "I like to _____ in the sun" pages for a classroom book titled *I Like the Sun!* Later read the book to the class and praise the children on their reading, writing, and illustrating abilities.

Reading

- Provide fiction and nonfiction books about stars and our solar system's sun. Be sure to include books of folk tales and legends in your reading area. Some books you can feature include *The Sun Is My Favorite Star* by Frank Asch, *Arrow to the Sun; A Pueblo Indian Tale* by Gerald McDermott, and *Sun Up, Sun Down* by Gail Gibbons.

- Enhance your reading area by providing some sunshine items like those in the dramatic play center (page 196). Provide a beach bag with sunglasses and beach towels for the children to use while relaxing and reading.

Abby writes from the predictable sentence strips that are in the writing center. She dictates, "The sun is in the sky."

Writing

- Create sentence strips using the word *sun*. The children can independently copy these sentences during center time. Predictable sentences help children to successfully read what is in front of them. To encourage early word recognition, use a yellow marker to write the word *sun*. Here are some predictable sentences you can include:

  The sun is yellow.
  The sun is hot.
  The sun is in the sky.

- At the writing area, include a Light Brite panel and some sun words on sheets of paper. Sun words can include *hot, sun, yellow, warm,* and *sky.* Children will enjoy illuminating their sun-filled words at this center.

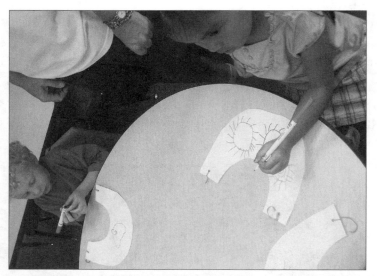

Abby creates her sun visor in the classroom. Later she and Caleb wear them to shade their eyes on the way home.

Dramatic Play

- Hang a handmade cardboard yellow sun in the dramatic play center to set the tone. Provide some fold-up lounge chairs, umbrellas, beach bags and towels, and a basket of sunglasses with some fun magazines and good books. Include an empty bottle of SPF sun lotion for the children to pretend to use. Show the children how to sit back and take it easy under a beach umbrella. They can relax and enjoy some recreational reading time in the sun.

Art

- Provide this fun, creative sun visor activity as a great reminder about the importance of protection from the sun. Precut white tag board in the shape of a sun visor for each child. Punch one hole at each end to add a rubber band or yarn fastener. Cut a rubber band or piece of yarn in half, and tie each half into a punched hole. Provide the children with crayons, markers, and colored pencils in warm, sunny colors: red, orange, and yellow. Let the children create abstract swirls and other sun-filled designs for their one-of-a-kind sun visor. When the children have finished decorating their visors, place them on their heads and tie the fastener ends together. Afterward take the children outside, proudly wearing their creative, sun-protective visors.

Music

- Explain to the children that they have been learning about a great light, our sun. Tell them they all have a bright light within them that they can shine to help warm others. Sing the classic song "This Little Light of Mine!" through once:

  This little light of mine,
  I'm going to let it shine.
  This little light of mine,
  I'm going to let it shine.
  This little light of mine,
  I'm going to let it shine.
  Let it shine, let it shine, let it shine!

  Now ask all the children to think of something they are good at and to include this in place of singing the line, "This little light of mine." For instance, if a child says she is good at riding bikes, the entire class would sing:

  Riding my bike,
  I'm going to let it shine.
  Riding my bike,
  I'm going to let it shine.
  Riding my bike,
  I'm going to let it shine.
  Let it shine, let it shine, let it shine!

  Continue singing the song until everyone has offered their light or talent to use in the lyric. Children will love hearing this version again and again as you celebrate everyone's unique shining.

Closing the Ready for the Sun Theme

Throughout your work with the Ready for the Sun activities, ask the children open-ended questions to increase their comprehension. In your group times, be sure to discuss interesting facts they have learned about sunshine. Here are some additional questions you can use during activities and to bring this theme to a close:

Why is the sun important?
What do you love most about the sun?
What do you know about the sun?

Summer Theme 3: Summer's Grass

Exploring Outside

Take the children outdoors to frolic through some summer grass. I always like the contrast of tall wild grass against recently cut grass. It brings all the senses to the forefront in regard to summer grass and its varieties. Finding an abundance of many types of grasses isn't likely to take much pursuit in the heart of summer. Encourage the children to sit in the grass and to feel it on their skin. Ask them open-ended questions about the grass, its freshness and texture:

The children immerse themselves in the tall grass.

What does the grass smell like?
What do you notice about the grass?
Do you see anything in it?
What else do you notice?

Show the children how to hold a flat piece of grass between their thumbs, which are pressed alongside each other. Explain that they should hold the grass firmly as they blow through the opening between their thumbs. Regardless of whether they succeed in making the loud whistling noise you are shooting for, the children will love to practice making a whistle of any kind.

Role Play Outside

While outdoors, explain to the children that they get to be grass. Ask them to move like grass flowing in the wind. Ask them questions while they pretend to be grasses:

How tall are you?
Do you have friends out here?
What kind of things do you see when you are grass?
Let me see what you look like.

Remind the children to use "I" statements when they respond. Questions and thoughts present never-ending possibilities. Often, children naturally share what their thoughts are in their pretend role.

Be sure to inquire using open-ended questions. Help children to develop their higher-level thinking skills by asking such questions:

What do you sound like?
How did you get here?
What do you like about yourself?
What is happening to you?

These are all fine open-ended questions for your role-playing time.

Braxtyn acts as if she is the rain and sprinkles rain on Nicholas, who is pretending to be the grass.

Involving Families: Studying Summer Grass at Home

Supply the children with some fun activities to do at home. Mention the activities in your weekly newsletter to families. Explain to families that the optional activities are provided for extra quality time together in nature and to involve them in their children's education. Explain that the children are learning about nature and summer grass. Describe the following nature activities for the families to enjoy at home:

- Send home a half sheet of paper that asks families to sit with their children in the grass near their home and come up with five descriptive words to send to school with their child. Make sure they include their name on the paper. Explain that you'll use the descriptive words in a group time circle activity while discussing grass.

- Ask families to play outside, spending time specifically in the grass. Have them send in a note describing what they did as a family. If they wish, they can send a photo along with the note. Explain to the families that you will create a chart of all the fun things families did in the grass in a language arts activity (see page 202).

Saige and Keefer decorate their grass head containers.

Integrating Nature: Studying Summer Grass in the Classroom

Children enjoy watching life and growth happen. Grass seed planted in a paper cup in the classroom grows in no time. Incorporating seed growing into your summer curriculum becomes a quick way to provide opportunities to appreciate new life and abundant growth for the children. They will also have such opportunities in the science and discovery, math, blocks and building, language arts, reading, writing, dramatic play, art, and music activities that follow.

Science and Discovery

Garrett plants his grass seed.

- Grow a groovy grass group. For this activity, you will need one paper cup for each child, markers, potting soil, and grass seed. Have the children write their names on their paper cups. The paper cup will represent their group grass member's head. Next, have them decorate their cup heads with the markers, drawing eyes, nose, ears, and mouth. To protect their artwork, cover the decorated area on each cup with clear packaging tape. Next, fill the cup three-quarters full of potting soil, and sprinkle grass seed on top. Top it off with a bit more soil and water. In only a few days, the children will be able to see their groovy grass group come to life—a cluster of them, all with full heads of hair. After a week or two, allow the children to give their grass members haircuts in a fun measuring and cutting math activity (see page 201).

Math

- After your groovy grass group grows some hair on their heads, move them from the science center to the math center. Put out some scissors, rulers, and small tape measures for some fun measuring and somewhat accurate cutting.

  Before having the children work at this center, create a sheet titled "Groovy Grass Measuring." Print enough so each child has one page. Include a space for the child's name and three areas for the children to record their measurements:

  My groovy grass hair measured _____ inches.
  I cut _____ inches from my groovy grass hair.
  My groovy grass head now measures _____ inches.

  Whether the measuring is precise or not, the children will be introduced to a measuring device and to experimenting with length dimensions.

- The writing center's live graph activity on page 203 is also a good math connection activity.

Blocks and Building

- Make a little putt-putt center in your blocks and building center. Lay down a small strip of artificial grass and outline it with blocks to serve as your putting barrier. Next, place a paper cup at one end and a golf ball and toy putter at the other. Children can count how many times they must putt to get their golf ball in the paper cup.

Language Arts

- Create a classroom chart (and later a big book) titled "A _____ Is a Graminivore." As a reminder for all you Latin minors from college, *graminivore* comes from the Latin word *graminis,* meaning grass, and *vorare* meaning to eat. Therefore, a graminivore is an animal that feeds mainly on grass. Horses, cattle, hippopotamuses, grasshoppers, and geese are all examples of graminivores.

- Create a classroom picture chart titled "A _____ Is a Graminivore." During large-group time, discuss the many animals that are considered graminivores, and remind children again and again that graminivores are animals that primarily feed on grass. Share pictures from a zoology website or library books to give the children examples. Ask each child to name her favorite graminivore. Record the children's responses next to their names on the chart.

- To make a big book, create on a blank 8½ x 11 inch page a sentence that reads, "A _____ is a graminivore." Be sure to include a space for a child's name on this page. Print enough copies so each child can have one. After participating in the large-group charting activity, children can use these pages to independently illustrate their favorite graminivore. Write young children's dictated responses on the blank line. Older children can copy their word from the chart. Those who need an extra challenge can phonetically write out their own word on the blank line.

- Collect and bind all of the children's papers into a classroom book titled *Graminivores!* Read the book to the class and praise the children on their reading, writing, and illustrating abilities. Children will love to go home and share the new vocabulary word *graminivore* with their families.

- For this next activity, use the information that families sent about playing outside together in the summer grass (see Involving Families, pages 199–200). Create a chart of all the fun things a family can do in the grass. Be sure to include any photos families sent. Children will love to describe how they played a baseball game, pitched a tent, or relaxed in lounge chairs together.

Reading

- Provide grass books for children to explore. Nonfiction books that depict the actual season and its attributes are an added bonus. Fiction books that feature tall grass will pique their interest as well. Some books you can feature include *In the Tall, Tall Grass* by Denise Fleming and *On Meadowview Street* by Henry Cole.

Writing

- Include premade sentence strips that include fun nature ideas for playing in grass. Read each sentence strip to the children. Post them in your writing center for children to independently copy from and illustrate from. Here are some sample sentences:

> I can look in the grass.
> I can tumble in the grass.
> I can lie in the grass and look up at the clouds.

- Create a live graph by asking children to stand behind the sentence strip about the activity they would like to do in the grass. For example, five children might stand behind the "look in the grass" strip, eight children might stand behind the "tumble in the grass" strip, and three might go behind the "lie in the grass and look up at the clouds" strip. During this activity, discuss graph terms, such as *most, least,* and *more than.* Continue to ask higher-level, critical-thinking questions, such as how many more children are at the "look in the grass" strip than at the "tumble in the grass" strip. Children will have to use their higher math abilities for interpreting the live graph. After this group activity, tape the strips at the writing center for the children to use while independently writing and illustrating.

- Later, after center time, take the children outside for some added fun activities in the grass. Bring magnifying glasses and let the children look in the grass, tumble in the grass, and lie back and watch the clouds.

Dramatic Play

- For your dramatic play center, create a banner that reads, "Families have fun in the summer grass." Allow children to recreate their families' fun activities in the dramatic play center. Use the chart from your language arts activity (page 202) about families playing outside together in the summer grass, and encourage the children to role-play all the different activities. If you can provide some props in a basket, such as a blanket to be used for a tent or for picnicking and other items mentioned on the chart, great! If not, don't worry—the children naturally know how to make believe in this popular play area.

Art

- Encourage the children to practice fine-motor skills while learning more about environmental art. Take a walk to look for some long, wild grass. When you find some, cut it at its base, keeping it as long as possible. Show the children how to braid three pieces together, using a simple under-over pattern. With the children, try to braid many strips of three long grass strands. Make many grass braid strips. Afterward, braid three strips together and continue to do so until you have braided all your strips. By blending straight sticks into your braid, you can create large triangular and square shapes. Hang these woven geometric grass pieces in a tree so everyone can marvel at your environmental art. Remind the children that environmental art dissipates back to the earth, so take a picture to preserve present beauty in your memories. Environmental art has a way of teaching children and adults the importance of the present moment.

Music

- Sing "The Grass Song" to the tune of "Bingo":

The Grass Song
I wonder what I'll find in the grass—
Flowers, honeybees, or ants?
G-r-a-s-s, g-r-a-s-s, g-r-a-s-s.
I wonder what I'll find in the grass.

I wonder what I'll find in the grass—
Weeds, dirt, or ladybugs?
G-r-a-s-s, g-r-a-s-s, g-r-a-s-s.
I wonder what I'll find in the grass.

Sing these two verses and then ask children what they think they will find in the grass. Use their ideas to make more verses. This will give the children power and ownership of the song, which they will enjoy singing again and again. Later, when you are all outdoors in the grass, remind children to sing "The Grass Song" as they notice all of the things in the summer grass.

Closing the Summer's Grass Theme

Throughout your work with the Summer's Grass activities, ask children questions to increase their comprehension. In your group times, be sure to discuss interesting facts they've learned about grass. Here are some additional questions you can use during activities and to bring this theme to a close:

Why is grass important?
What can you find in the grass?
What do you like about grass?

Summer Theme 4: Relaxing with the Sand

Exploring Outside

Unless you live near a beach or a sandy-bottomed water source, you may have difficulty finding sand just outside your classroom door. Thanks to children's love of this tactile granular material, though, you can buy sand at hardware stores in fifty-pound bags or larger for just a few dollars. The children's merriment at playing in sand certainly outweighs the cost, a million to one.

Sand is a perfect inexpensive material to incorporate into your summer curriculum. Once you have it at your fingertips, take children outdoors on the ideal summer day for some sifting and observing. Pour the sand onto a vinyl tablecloth and include some sand toys for fun. Children will enjoy writing their names, creating paths, and sifting the sand through their fingers.

While the children are sifting sand through their hands, ask open-ended questions, such as these:

What does it feel like?
What do you notice about it?
How is it different from soil?
What else do you notice?

Role Play Outside

While outdoors, explain to the children that they get to be the sand. They can pretend they're on a beach, be a wet sand castle, or be dry and sifting through the fingers of children. (When I teach yoga, during my cool-down relaxation segment, I ask participants to relax their muscles and bodies by "becoming like sand.") Begin by saying to the children, "Tell me about yourself!" Ask the children to describe themselves. Be sure to have them use "I" terms when describing themselves as sand. After listening to their answers, ask them additional open-ended questions:

How did you get here?
What do you like about yourself?
What do others like about you?
How do you feel being in children's hands?
What do you like to do?

Involving Families: Studying Sand at Home

Supply the children with some fun activities to do at home. Mention the activities in your weekly newsletter to families. Explain to families that the optional activities are provided for extra quality time together in nature and to involve them in their children's education. Explain that in this summer season, the children are learning about sand. Describe the following nature activities for the families to enjoy at home:

- Ask families to send a beach bag with their child to school. They should include these items in the bag: a beach towel, water bottle, and a good book to relax with. Explain to families that children will be using their items during your "Relaxing with the Sand" theme in independent center time in your reading center.

- Ask families for help in completing a classroom graph titled "Has your family been to a sandy beach?" Send home a half sheet of paper with the question, "Has your family been to a sandy beach?" Be sure to include a space for the family to write their name and yes or no check boxes. When all responses have been sent back to school, create a math graph on large chart paper by taping all the responses to either the yes or no column (see math activity, page 207).

Integrating Nature: Studying Sand in the Classroom

Pour sand you've purchased or collected into buckets or a bag and cart it back to the classroom for more integrative fun and learning. The children will be able to get their hands in sand while working on the science and discovery, dramatic play, and math activities. The children will also be delving into sand in the writing area and creating some sandy art too.

Science and Discovery

- Explain to the children that sand is a natural granular material made up of finely divided rock and mineral particles. (Review your spring Finding Stones theme, page 169, as the children learn more about sand.) Put scoops, measuring cups, beakers, containers, sifters, shovels, and other sand toys in a small, deep sand tray or other pan in the science and discovery center. Model for the children how to fill one measuring cup and pour sand into long beakers and other containers. Ask questions that initiate play, such as "How many cups do you think it will take to fill this container?" Ask other questions to encourage critical thinking, such as "What can you do with the sand?" and "How could you use this instrument or container—what else could you do with it?"

- After all the children have circulated through this center, pour water on the sand for a different type of texture and consistency.

- After all the children have circulated through the wet sand play, allow the sand to dry out, then bring attention to any differences in the texture.

Math

- Make sand weights. Use a funnel to fill up different sizes and colors of balloons with sand. Tie off each full balloon, making sure you have an assortment of sand weights. Using a permanent marker, label each sand balloon weight by its color. Include a scale and items to weigh, such as a block, a book, and other classroom items. Allow the children to freely explore in this area. They will enjoy weighing the different items by using the various colors of sand-filled balloons as weights. Ask questions that initiate play, such as "How much did the book weigh? How did you figure it out?" Children might say that the book weighed one red and one yellow balloon. When children verbalize how they figured out their math problem, they use their higher-thinking skills.

- As a group, create a graph titled "Has your family been to a sandy beach?" When families have all sent their beach question responses back to school (see Involving Families, page 206), create a math graph on large chart paper by taping all the responses to either the yes or no column. Discuss the graph terms *most, least,* and *equal to.* Don't forget to ask this higher-thinking math-skill question: "How many more yes (or no) responses are there than no (or yes) responses?"

Blocks and Building

- Discuss picnics at a sandy beach, and ask your little builders to craft some interesting picnic tables and benches. Provide pictures of wooden picnic tables and chairs, and let the children create. Add a small picnic basket filled with play food and paper plates to complete the fun. If you do not have a large supply of blocks, create a mini version of picnic table and benches and supply mini toy dolls for an imaginary sandy beach picnic.

Language Arts

- Begin a classroom chart titled "I went for a walk on a sandy beach. . . ." Before doing this large group activity, discuss the story structure concepts of *beginning*, *middle*, and *end*. Talk enthusiastically about stories having powerful beginning, middle, and end sections. Have the children contribute to this story by dividing the activity into five teaching-time group sessions:

    Day 1: In the first group time, focus on the beginning of the story, concentrating on characters and setting. Label your chart paper "Beginning of the story." Ask children for ideas and chart all of their responses.

    Day 2: During your next group time, focus on the middle of the story and coming up with an obstacle or problem the characters face. Label this chart paper "Middle of the story," and chart all of the children's ideas for obstacles or problems.

    Day 3: For your third group activity, focus on the ending of the story—how it resolves. Label this chart paper "End of story." Chart all of the children's ideas for a story ending.

    Day 4: Review your chart papers for the story's beginning, middle, and end. Now, as a group, write the story on another piece of chart paper. Begin with the sentence "I went for a walk on a sandy beach. . . ." Choose at least one idea from each chart to make the story. Write each sentence in a different color. (Groups of children will use the colors to refer to the sentences for their Day 5 illustrations.)

    Day 5: Have children work cooperatively in groups of two or three. Each group will illustrate one colored sentence from Day 4's chart paper. Be sure to record which group is illustrating which sentence. Cut each colored sentence from the chart paper and glue it to the cooperative group's artwork.

Close this lesson by binding together the illustrated pages in a book, and read it to the entire class. Celebrate their knowledge of beginning, middle, and end story structure.

Reading

- Provide fiction and nonfiction books on the topic of sand and beaches for children to explore. Some books you can feature include *Sea, Sand, Me!* by Patricia Hubbell and *The Sandcastle Contest* by Robert Munsch.

- Include beach towels, sunglasses, umbrellas, and beach chairs to encourage reading the whole summer through.

- Include the language arts activity's *I Went for a Walk on a Sandy Beach. . . .* book in the reading center for children to revisit when they wish.

Writing

- Include a few trays of sand at your writing center for the children to use to practice writing their names and other summer words. Before introducing this activity, make a picture chart listing as many summer words as possible, making sure you begin with *sand* and *sun*. You do not have to be an art teacher to make a picture chart. Simple stick drawings and easy doodles next to the words will do. Allow the children to think about all the key attributes of summer, and add these ideas to your picture chart. Hang the picture chart near your writing center for the children to copy from. As they independently write in the sand at this center, ask the children what words they are writing. They undoubtedly will remember every summer word from your clear-cut pictures. As they share with you which word they are writing, enthusiastically praise them on becoming strong readers *and* writers!

- Include large strips of sandpaper at your writing center. Model how to put the sandpaper under blank paper and practice writing the summer words from the picture chart. Tactile learners will enjoy their writing even more!

Dramatic Play

- Let the children make an imaginary world. Supply two sand trays (preferably each 2 or 3 inches deep) on which the children can base their imaginary world. Provide a tray full of miniatures—mini dinosaurs, trees, animals, people, shells, rocks, aquarium items, toys, or virtually any small thing. Have two groups of children cooperate to create an imaginary world on the two sand trays. When both groups have finished, ask each group to tell you about its created world. To draw out the children's use of language and critical thinking, feel free to make factual observations and ask nonjudgmental questions, such as "I notice there are only shells and plants in your world—why is that?" Continue to facilitate while both groups compare and contrast their two worlds.

Art

- Create some process and abstract sandy beach art by giving the children a piece of tagboard, watercolor paints, newspaper, a bowl of sand, and glue in a squeezable bottle. Invite them to write their names on the back of the tagboard and then turn it over and place it on top of the newspaper. Begin by painting an ocean, using watercolors over the entire tagboard page in hues of blue, green, and purple. After the paint dries, let the children squeeze swirls and designs of glue onto their colored tagboard. While the glue is still wet, they can pick up some sand from the bowl and gently sift it onto the glue design. Allow the design to dry slightly before you gently tip the paper and carefully shake the remainder of the sand onto the newspaper. Let the artwork dry completely before you send it home with the children. Applaud them for their abstract sandy beach artwork.

Music

- Sing "The Sand Song" to the tune of "Row, Row, Row Your Boat":

  The Sand Song
  Sand, sand on the beach
  In between my toes.
  This is what it feels like with
  Sand between my toes.

  After singing, ask the children, "What do you think it feels like to have sand between your toes?" Give every child an opportunity to share a descriptive word. Then sing this verse:

Sand, sand on the beach
In between my teeth.
This is what it feels like with
Sand between my teeth.

After singing, ask children, "What do you think it feels like to have sand between your teeth?" Give every child an opportunity to share a descriptive word. Then sing this next verse:

Sand, sand on the beach
All through my hair.
This is what it feels like with sand
All through my hair.

After singing, ask children, "What do you think it feels like to have sand through your hair?" Give every child an opportunity to share a descriptive word.

Make up other verses, such as "In my food" and "In my shoes" as you draw out descriptive words from the children's vocabulary.

Closing the Relaxing with the Sand Theme

Throughout your work with the Relaxing with the Sand activities, ask children questions to increase their comprehension. In your group times, be sure to discuss interesting things they noticed about sand. Here are some additional questions you can use during activities and to bring this theme to a close:

What do you like best about sand?
What do you find interesting about sand?
Is there anything new you learned about sand?

Summer Theme 5: Busy Honeybees

Exploring Outside

After discussing honeybees indoors, take children outdoors to view honeybees in action. As in the Summer's Insects activity (page 184), remind the children that they are looking for bees, which are flying insects. Because they are insects, bees have a head, thorax (chest), abdomen, and six legs. Remind the children that they should not get too close to the bees because the insects could sting if they are provoked. It is better to love them and appreciate their contribution to nature from afar. Explain that bees can usually be found busily working over clover or wildflowers. When the children have spotted some bees, ask them a few open-ended questions to help them focus on these busy insect creatures:

What do you think the bees are doing?
How long do you think they stay at one flower?
Do you think they rest?
How do you think they communicate with each other?
How do they eat and sleep?
How do they remember where they live?
What else do you notice?

The potential for questions is vast.

Role Play Outside

While outdoors, explain to the children that they get to be busy little honeybees. Ask the children to fly about, buzzing from one flower to the next, as they make believe they are bees. Begin by saying, "Let me see you fly" and "Let me hear what you sound like." Encourage the children to use "I" statements in their responses when they are pretending to be bees—for example, "I am a bee, buzzing around."

Ask open-ended questions to strengthen the children's language abilities and develop their thought processes. Questions might include some of these:

Which flower do you like best?
What are you so busy doing?
What is the best thing about being you?
Do you ever sting, and why?

Involving Families: Studying Honeybees at Home

Supply the children with some fun activities to do at home. Mention the activities in your weekly newsletter to families. Explain to families that the optional activities are provided for extra quality time together in nature and to involve them in their children's education. Explain that the children are learning more about insects; this time the classroom's focus is on honeybees and their important work. Describe the following nature activities for the families to enjoy at home:

- Tell families that you would appreciate their help with this valuable fun activity for home: cooperative work. Just as the busy honeybees work together to create important things in nature, so families need to work together cooperatively for jobs to be done efficiently and well. When done supportively, magnificent things can be accomplished, just as in the honeybee's world. Ask families to work together on any project around the home. Anything from cleaning the garage together to picking up the yard to planting a flower or rock garden would be a great family task.

- Send home a premade cutout of a yellow hexagon. Explain that all the hexagons should be returned to school by a certain date to be put on a bulletin board. After the families complete their household project(s) together, have their children draw a picture in the hexagon of the work they cooperatively completed as a family. Parents or guardians should help write on the hexagon what they did, such as "We cleaned the garage together" or "We picked up the backyard." When the children return their family's hexagons to school, put all of them together on a bulletin board titled "Busy Family Bees Cooperatively Work Together." Children will love viewing the bulletin board, and families who visit or volunteer in the classroom will proudly notice their contribution to the classroom's comb honey bulletin board.

Integrating Nature: Studying Honeybees in the Classroom

Honeybees are best left outdoors. However, there are many ice-cream stands and honey businesses that have indoor glass beehives for real-life viewing. Check on the Internet or with your local Chamber of Commerce for any neighboring glass honey beehives. Many would welcome you if you chose to bring your class on a field trip to view this wonderful piece of nature. Included next are honeybee ideas for your science and discovery, math, blocks and building, language arts, reading, writing, dramatic play, art, and music areas.

Science and Discovery

- Include pictures of honeybees at work in their hive and on flowers. Share honeybee products with the children. Show the children beeswax, beeswax lotion, comb honey, and different varieties of jar honey, such as clover, wildflower, and any other light floral honey. Include pictures of clover, wildflowers, or another honey flowers on index cards folded in half. Place these in front of the honey jars to expand children's comprehension of honey bees' products. Keep the items in the science center for independent center time.

- Allow the children to try beeswax lotion on their hands. Discuss its scent and texture. Using a honeybee-related product will help children develop a deeper appreciation for these flying friends.

Math

- If you have a tub of geometrical sorting shapes, put them out for the children to explore. If you are unable to find any shapes, make your geometrical sorting shapes on the computer. Print hexagons on yellow paper, rhomboid shapes on red paper, triangles on green, squares on orange, and diamonds on blue paper. A full array of shapes are best; allow the children to uncover new discoveries about the shapes. Focus on the hexagon shape, and show children that comb honey is in the shape of minihexagons. Make your own comb honey assemblage by putting many hexagon shapes together. Show children how putting two square shapes side by side with triangles on the bottom and top creates a hexagon too. Allow the children to freely explore making geometric shapes from the other shapes.

- For more math fun, refer to the art activity, which focuses on geometric shapes, on page 217.

Blocks and Building

- Bring back your Summer's Insects blocks and other materials to use in this Busy Honeybees theme. Once again, include letter development in your building area by showing the children how to spell the word *Insects,* using various curved and straight blocks. Provide a poster with the word *Insects* in a simple block font. Show the children how to use curved blocks for making curvy letters, such

Christine and Brittany work together comparing, sorting, and examining math manipulatives.

as *c* and *s,* and how to use straight blocks for making straight letters, such as *t* and *I.* Include a bucket of plastic toy insects for the children to place along the top of the block word. As you remind children that honeybees are insects, ask them, "What do all those letters spell?" During their independent practice, praise them, saying, "Wow, you spelled the word *Insects.* Great spelling!"

  As a variation to this theme, show the children how to make hexagons (a geometric shape of six sides) using straight blocks of equal lengths. To expand children's comprehension, reflect with them on the Busy Honeybees math and art hexagon activities.

Language Arts

- As a large group, write a descriptive list that uses the senses. Explain to the children that great writers use their senses in their writing to help their readers feel as though they are actually there in the story. Explain that they can write about honeybees using their senses. At the top of chart paper, write "Honeybees." Ask the children to describe what a honeybee looks and sounds like. Next, write the heading "Comb Honey" on the chart. Ask the children to describe what comb honey looks and tastes like. Write the next heading, "Beeswax Lotion." Ask the children to describe what beeswax lotion looks and feels like. Finish by reading all the descriptions you created as a class. Praise the children for using their senses well in their writing.

Reading

- Provide bee-related nonfiction books that show close-up pictures of honeybees at work. Be sure to include books that show insect body parts (head, thorax, and abdomen). Fiction books that feature the behavior of busy bees, and more important, cooperatively working together, will be enjoyable for the children as well. Some books you can feature include *Honey Bees* by Martha E. H. Rustad and *The Magic School Bus: Inside a Beehive* by Joanna Cole.

Writing

- Provide sentence strips that include *honeybee*. Create three predictable sentences for writing:

  1. A honeybee gives us honey.
  2. A honeybee gives us beeswax.
  3. A honeybee gives us comb honey.

  Children will be able to view and copy these strips in the writing center. To encourage early word recognition and one-to-one reading correspondence, use a colored marker to write *honeybee*. Including pictures for children with emergent reading skills will help them greatly. Allow the children to write and create at this literacy station.

Dramatic Play

- Revisit the Summer's Insect theme. Turn your dramatic play center into a summertime nature center. As before, bring out a tree or plant and some real flowers to place around your center, making the greenery as lush and abundant as possible to get the full summer effect. If these items are not readily available, use silk flowers and an artificial tree, or homemade flowers and a cardboard painted tree.

  Again, hang the insect necklaces that you used from your Summer's Insects theme, making sure to include an equal number of flying insects and crawling insects. If you haven't already, be sure to include honeybees and ants, since we will revisit this play area with our upcoming Picnic Ants theme (pages 223–24). To enhance children's classification and identification skills, write the sentence "I am a honeybee" or "I am an ant" below the original sentences "I am a flyer" or "I am a crawler." Children can choose which particular insect they want to be by wearing the corresponding necklace.

To develop children's inquiry and critical-thinking skills, ask them open-ended questions, such as "Why did you choose to be the honeybee [or whichever insect necklace they are wearing]?" and "What do you like best about being a honeybee?" Include some honeybee posters and honeycomb as you tune in more to your Busy Honeybees theme.

Art

- Connect the math activity to this art lesson by providing small paper hexagons, triangles, squares, and other geometric shapes. Give the children a blank piece of white construction paper, a glue stick, and access to all the geometric shapes. Tell them to become busy little bees and create any picture or design they would like to make from the shapes provided. Some children might make a house from squares and triangles. Others might make a beehive from hexagons. Let the children use their imagination and create something special.

Music

- Write the lyrics to "A Honeybee" on chart paper. Adding pictures for the words *honeybee, beeswax, comb honey,* and *honey* will help the children with word-to-word reading correspondence.

  Next, sing "A Honeybee" to the tune of "Row, Row, Row Your Boat":

  A Honeybee
  A honeybee gives us things.
  This is what they do.
  A honeybee makes the honey,
  Beeswax, and comb honey too.

- As a transitional activity, play Rimsky-Korsakov's music "Flight of the Bumblebee" while the children, as bees, busily pick up after center time. They will enjoy moving about quickly, as if they are flying like bees. Pickup time will move along faster and the transition will be more enjoyable for everyone.

Closing the Busy Honeybees Theme

Throughout your work with the Busy Honeybees activities, ask children questions to increase their comprehension. In your group times, be sure to discuss why honeybees are important. Here are some additional questions you can use during activities and to bring this theme to a close:

Why are honeybees important?
What do they give us?
How do bees help plants?

Summer Theme 6:
Picnic Ants

Exploring Outside

It is wonderful that virtually all children go through a bug-loving stage. It must be their innate fascination with life. It is also wonderful that summer is the perfect time for observing these little creatures—the bugs, that is.

You simply can't have summer without a picnic in the park, and at a picnic, ants will likely come marching by for a visit. Gather some simple munchies in a picnic basket and a classic red-and-white tablecloth, a blanket, or whatever summer throw you have handy, and take the children outdoors to view these tiny life forms in action. Remind the children that ants are insects, bugs with a head, thorax (chest), abdomen, and six legs. As with your other summer bug activities, bring along magnifying glasses for a closer look.

Once you've found ants, ask open-ended questions such as these to point out the ants' characteristics:

What do you notice about the ants?
What do you think they are doing?
Do you think they get tired?
How do they know how to find the food?
How do they eat?
What else do you notice?

The potential for questions is endless.

Role Play Outside

While outdoors, explain to the children that they get to be ants. Ask them to show you how they crawl, how they form lines, and how they carry things.

Begin by saying, "Tell me about yourself!" Remind children to use "I" statements while they are pretending to be the ants—for example, "I am a small ant. I can also carry heavy loads on my back."

Asking open-ended questions about their ant antics gives children a chance to use their best language skills and develop reflection:

Where do you live?
What do you do?
Where do you put the food in your home?
Show me what you look like.
Do you live with your family?
What do you do for fun?
What is the best thing about being you?
Are you ever afraid of being so small in the world?

Involving Families: Studying Ants at Home

Supply the children with some fun activities to do at home. Mention the activities in your weekly newsletter to families. Explain to families that the optional activities are provided for extra quality time together in nature and to involve them in their children's education. Explain that the children are learning about tiny creatures: ants. Describe the following nature activities for the families to enjoy at home:

- Invite families to add meaningful conversation minutes to their week by going on a picnic together. Ask them to observe if any ants visited their picnic area during their special family time together. Provide a half sheet of paper with the question, "Did ants visit you on your family picnic?" Have them check a yes or no box and return the paper to school. Tell families that all of their responses will be used to create a graph in the classroom.

Integrating Nature: Studying Ants in the Classroom

Ants are one of the first tiny insects that many children encounter. The children will enjoy viewing an ant farm in the science and discovery activity, describing ants they found on their family picnic, and participating in ant-themed activities.

Science and Discovery

- Buy and display an ant farm in your science area. Find one that includes a transparent side through which the children can view the daily workings of ants. This allows the children to examine live insects crawling around in the classroom—or, as many teachers prefer to note, crawling around in a secured, tightly covered small container within the classroom. Include magnifying glasses for children to get a closer look at these tiny insects. Also be sure to display posters with close-up pictures of ants in action. Include a picture of an ant with labels indicating its body parts: head, thorax, and abdomen.

Math

- Children will make Ants on a Log snack at the language arts center (page 222) to enjoy on a picnic place mat they will create as an art activity (page 224). While they enjoy this nutritious snack, they can practice some math skills too! Give all of the children a short stalk of celery. Have them use a craft stick to spread peanut butter or cream cheese in the celery's crevice. Next, have them measure their stalks in the number of raisins (or "ants," as they will love to call them) that fit on top. Let's say one child's stalk measures thirteen ants. Instruct the children to place a portion of their "ants" to the left side then leave a space, and then put the rest of the "ants" to the right. Ask them to count each portion. For example, say the same child's stalk has seven ants on the left and six ants on the right. Ask the children to add 7 + 6 = _____. Ants on a Log is a fine introduction to early adding skills.

- As a class, create a math graph from the "Did ants visit you on your family picnic?" information sheets that families sent in (see Involving Families, page 220). On chart paper, title the graph "Did ants visit you on your family picnic?" Make two columns on the chart, one for yes and one for no answers. With the children, tape all the families' responses in the appropriate yes or no column. Discuss the results and the graph terms *most, least,* and *how many more than.*

Blocks and Building

- Continue using the Summer's Insects and Busy Honeybees blocks and building materials during this Picnic Ants theme. Once again, foster letter development by asking the children to spell the word *Insects* using various curved and straight blocks.

Provide a poster with the word *Insects* in a simple block font. Show the children how to use curved blocks for making curvy letters, such as *c* and *s,* and how to use straight blocks for making straight letters, such as *t* and *I.* Include a bucket of plastic toy insects for the children to place along the top of the block word. As you remind children that ants are insects, ask them, "What do all those letters spell?" Praise them, saying, "Wow, you spelled the word *Insects.* Great spelling!"

• Invite the children to make tunnels using blocks. Discuss with them how ants build ant colonies underground.

Language Arts

• Connect this language arts activity with the math activity (page 221) by scripting a simple recipe for Ants on a Log. Begin by showing the children different recipes, and draw their attention to each recipe's numbered steps. Explain that recipe directions tell us how to make something correctly. Further clarify that by including numbered steps, a recipe shows us how to do something in order. Tell children they will soon have a chance to make an Ants on a Log snack, but to do so, they will need to follow the steps in a recipe. Title the chart paper "Ants on a Log." Then write these steps on the chart, discussing them with the children as you do:

Ants on a Log

1. Wash hands and wash a stalk of celery.

2. Cut the celery stalk in four equal lengths.

3. Spread each celery stalk with peanut butter or cream cheese.

4. Put raisins on each celery stalk.

5. Eat and enjoy with friends!

Children will actually make this recipe, as well as using the raisin "ants" to practice counting and adding in the math activity on page 221. If you do the language arts and math activities with the children after they've completed the art activity on page 224, they'll have a classic red-and-white place mat to eat their snack on.

Reading

- Provide insect books in the reading center for children to explore. Make sure that ants are featured in the book's topics and some of their titles. Providing children with nonfiction books that show actual insects and their body parts will be great for all the young children who are still in their bug fascination stage. Fiction books and ant fables that include this popular insect as characters will pique children's interests as well. Some books you can feature include *Hey, Little Ant* by Philip M. Hoose and Hannah Hoose and *One Hundred Hungry Ants* by Elinor J. Pinczes.

Writing

- Ants are known for their hard work and cooperative colonies. Discuss with the children these social aspects of ants. Connect these qualities to human experience and what we can learn from ants socially. Use this as a writing activity in which the classroom is compared to an ant's life, full of wonderful hard work and cooperation. Make a bulletin board titled "[Teacher's name]'s hardworking and cooperative helpers!" During circle time, ask children to share what they do to contribute, cooperate, and work in the classroom. Record their responses on chart paper. Afterward, the children can make an ant from a black circle and oval cutouts. They can make antennas by curling small black construction paper strips using a pencil. After the ants are glued, curled, and created, staple each child's artwork to the bulletin board. Teachers can record younger children's responses on an index card and include it on the ant's back, just as if they are carrying a load. Modify the lesson for older children by having them write out their responses phonetically on an index card.

Dramatic Play

- Continue the Summertime Nature study theme from the Summer's Insects and Busy Honeybees dramatic play center. This time, include a picnic basket, play food, and a red-and-white checked tablecloth for little ones to create a picnic. Allow a small group of children to spread out a picnic around your plants and flowers.

  Again, hang the necklaces from your Summer's Insects theme in this area, making sure to include flying and crawling insects. While some children picnic, others can choose which particular insect they want to be by wearing the corresponding necklace.

Watch those ants! They will want to march by that beautiful picnic area, taking the peanut butter and honey sandwiches on their backs!

Art

• Make a picnic place mat by weaving together red and white strips of construction paper. If you feel your students are too young for a weaving paper activity, create a premade paper on the computer with rows and columns of squares. Copy it onto 9 x 12 inch white construction paper. Students can paint every other square red, thus creating the traditional red-and-white patterned place mat. Notice how art and math lessons are integrated beautifully in this activity. Laminate the place mats. The children can use them to enjoy their Ants on a Log treat during your Math activity on page 221. (They'll learn about the recipe to make this snack during the language arts activity on page 222.)

Music

• Sing the classic, all-time favorite "The Ants Go Marching" as a group. Act out the song by marching and singing together. Be sure to hold up the correct number of fingers for each verse. Bring up the term *rhyming*, explaining that rhyming basically means "sounding alike."

> **The Ants Go Marching**
> The ants go marching one by one, hurrah, hurrah!
> The ants go marching one by one, hurrah, hurrah!
> The ants go marching one by one,
> The little one stops *[insert something that rhymes with one]*
> And they all go marching down to the ground,
> To get out of the rain!
> Boom, boom, boom, boom, boom, boom, boom, boom!
>
> The ants go marching two by two, hurrah, hurrah!
> The ants go marching two by two, hurrah, hurrah!
> The ants go marching two by two,
> The little one stops *[insert something that rhymes with two]*
> And they all go marching down to the ground,
> To get out of the rain!
> Boom, boom, boom, boom, boom, boom, boom, boom!

Continue singing the song and coming up with rhymes for each number through 10.

Closing the Picnic Ants Theme

Throughout your work with the Picnic Ants activities, ask children questions to increase their comprehension. In your group times, be sure to discuss the ant colonies and cooperative work. Here are some additional questions you can use during activities and to bring this theme to a close:

What do you know about ants?
How do ants work together?

Summer Theme 7: Bloomin' Flowers

Exploring Outside

Now that summer's abundance is as full as it gets, guide the children on a community walk to view all the beautiful flowers of the season. Be sure to take along your camera to photograph flowers at businesses, homes, in roadside landscapes, and wherever else you see gorgeous blooms. Afterward, head back to the school grounds to photograph your own charming landscape. Be sure to check out the perimeters to find some stunning wildflowers too.

Bring some magnifying glasses and allow the children to look closely at the buds and blossoms. Explain a flower's delicacy to them and remind them that they should only look—no picking flowers at this time.

Just as in your observations of spring's First Flowers theme, ask these open-ended questions:

What do you see inside in the flower?
What do you notice?
What else do you see?
What does the flower smell like?
What does it feel like?
What else do you notice?

These and other questions will help children to examine nature's blooms more closely. Remind children about the delicacy of flowers. Doing so will help them develop respect and admiration for nature.

Role Play Outside

While outdoors, explain to the children that they get to be their favorite summer flower. Ask them to show you their beauty. Begin by saying, "Tell me about yourself!" Children should use "I" statements when telling you about being their favorite blooms. Use open-ended questions to stimulate the children's development of higher-level thinking: "How did you get here?" always creates a fine opening and generates some imaginative dialogue. Other helpful questions include these:

What do you look like?
What is your favorite part about being here?
What do you like about yourself?
What is your purpose?
Tell me more about yourself.

Involving Families: Studying Bloomin' Flowers at Home

Supply the children with some fun activities to do at home. Mention the activities in your weekly newsletter to families. Explain to families that the optional activities are provided for extra quality time together in nature and to involve them in their children's education. Explain that the children are learning about summer's bloomin' flowers. Describe the following nature activities for them to enjoy at home:

- Take a summer walk together and appreciate all the flowers you observe.

- Share with each other what your favorite flower is and why.

- Talk about the importance of flowers, how honeybees make honey from clover and wildflowers.

- Explain that pollination is an important aspect of flowers' lives.

- Ask families with flower gardens to share a flower bloom or two with the class. The flowers will be put in the science and discovery center for the children to observe and in the reading center for enjoyment while they read books about flowers.

Integrating Nature: Studying Bloomin' Flowers in the Classroom

Brighten your summer classroom by bringing a few flowers back from your Exploring Outside segment. Trim a few of the summer wildflowers for use in flowery projects in science and discovery, math, blocks and building, language arts, reading, writing, dramatic play, art, and music activities.

Science and Discovery

- Include large pictures or posters of summer flowers in your science area. Lilies, roses, and daisies make wonderful summer pictures. Use one flower vase per each of the three types of summer flowers. Provide magnifying glasses for the children to examine the flowers more closely. Ask about the flowers' similarities and differences. You can explain briefly the difference between annual and perennial flowers and plants. Mostly the children will enjoy smelling, gently touching, and appreciating the flowers' beauty.

- Talk to children about scents and using their sense of smell. Try this activity for developing children's thinking skills and strengthening their sense of smell. Spray two cotton balls lightly with the same floral perfume and place each one in a recycled film canister or other small plastic container with a lid. Poke a small hole in each lid so children will smell the scent when they hold a container near their noses. Label the bottom of one container A and the other a for matching purposes.

  Now spray two more cotton balls lightly with a different kind of floral perfume or scented oil. Place each cotton ball in its own container and label the bottom, this time with B or b for matching purposes. Do the same with the third floral perfume or oil, and label these containers C and c. Leave all six containers in the science area with a key sheet labeled "Aa = [type of perfume]," "Bb = [its perfume]," and "Cc = [its perfume]." Children will have fun smelling the scents and trying to match up the corresponding pairs.

Math

- Provide an everlasting bouquet of flower patterning options by supplying the math center with bunches of silk flowers in a variety of colors. Cut off the top petal parts of a variety of silk flowers and create a fun patterning station for the children. Include strips of white paper with simple A-B, A-B-C, A-B-B, A-A-B-B, and other patterns. No need for glue—keep these strips as your master patterns, and children can do this activity again and again. They will gain much-needed early math skills by replicating patterns with the petals. This hands-on flower patterning is perfect for your early math learners and ideal for advanced young mathematicians as they create independently. Here are some patterning examples to get you started:

A-B-A-B-A-B-A-B-A-B-A-B

A-B-C-A-B-C-A-B-C-A-B-C

A-B-B-A-B-B-A-B-B-A-B-B

A-A-B-B-A-A-B-B-A-A-B-B

Save the pattern strips to use for your Bloomin' Flowers music activity.

Blocks and Building

- Revisit the fun flower bed building center that the children enjoyed in the spring season's First Flowers theme. During that theme, the children created rectangular flower beds in your block area. This time, ask your little landscapers to craft other shapely flower beds, making circular, oval, and square ones. Provide bright silk flowers to plant, and bring back a tub of those fun packing peanuts to serve as soil. Add some gardening gloves and play shovels, and watch the children design beautifully shaped flower beds in which to display summer's bloomin' flowers.

Language Arts

- Make a flower picture book. Print the colored photos from the Exploring Outside activity and glue each picture to an 11 x 18 inch sheet of construction paper. Place all the pages together and title the book *Summer's Bloomin' Flowers*. Bind the pages using metal rings or yarn ties to create a large picture book. Present the book to the children, who can review the pictures independently, since the book has no printed words.

- Next, teach about picture captions and how they provide valuable information for readers. Suggest to the children that they could make the *Bloomin' Flowers* wordless big book more interesting by adding captions. Begin by prompting their memories of their Exploring Outdoors summer walk through the community and school grounds. Then work with them to devise a caption for each picture. Finish by having a second look at your classroom big book, this time reading each caption.

Reading

- Provide books about flowers galore. Again, make sure plenty show colorful close-ups of flowers' parts, such as leaves, petals, sepals, stamens, and pistils. Some books you can feature include *From Seed to Plant* by Gail Gibbons and *The Empty Pot* by Demi.

- Repeat the reading center décor that you used for spring's First Flowers theme, but this time spruce it up to be more summer-like and include summer blooms. Make this center a flowery, aromatic place to enjoy a good book. Include vases of summery flowers. Provide wildflowers gathered during your outings and include any blooms that families sent in. The children will be able to look at and smell them as they read about flowers and flowering trees. They will enjoy sitting back and smelling the roses (or peonies, lilies, or any other summer flower) while reading books.

Writing

- Teach the children about writing lists. Explain that lists are simple ways of remembering things you want to recall. With the children, create a list on chart paper of all the flowers they saw on the Exploring Outside community walk. Include categories for colors of flowers, types of flowers, and anything else they want to remember from their time together in the community. To encourage color name recognition, use corresponding color markers to write the color words. When the list is complete, hang the chart paper in your writing center, where the children can view it easily. Here is a sample list showing the types of items you might include on your chart paper:

    Colored flowers we saw on our walk:
    - red
    - purple
    - pink
    - yellow

Types of flowers we picked for our classroom:
- daisies
- clovers
- pansies

Things we noticed about flowers:
- petals
- stems
- leaves
- roots
- colors
- texture

Where we saw flowers:
- stores
- bank
- homes
- waterway
- flowerpots
- school entranceway

Dramatic Play

- Just as you did in spring, turn your dramatic play center into a garden center. Children will enjoy this center once again. Include play shovels and hoes. Put out an abundance of silk flowers and plastic pails for the children to make bouquets. Be sure to include watering cans, sprayers, mini plastic pots, and gardening gloves. The children will love pretending they work at the local garden center.

Art

- Make colorful summer flowers. Paint with watercolor on a coffee filter, using pretty summer rainbow colors. When the paint has dried, bunch up the filter in the middle and staple it to a long green piece of construction paper to represent the flower's stem. Use green tempera to paint the children's hands so they can make handprints on a small piece of green construction paper. When the paper has dried, cut out each handprint, using each one for the flower's leaves. Glue one leaf to each side of the stem. Afterward, review the basic parts of a flower with the children, focusing on petal, stem, leaves, and roots.

Music

- From your Math activity, use the pattern strips for a short patterned music lesson. Include the strips on chart paper during a brief group time. Tell the children to think of a different sound for *a*, *b*, and *c*. For example, they may choose a very soft sound for *a*, a middle tone for *b*, and a loud tone for *c*. Say each letter using the soft, regular, and loud tones to help them practice and remember. Next, using the pointer, point to each letter on a pattern strip. Sing together, using the corresponding tones of soft, regular, and loud. Repeat the pattern several times.

  You could also provide a hand motion along with each sound. For instance, while saying the soft *a*, children put their hands on their knees. When singing the regular *b* sound, children put their hands on their shoulders. And when loudly expressing the *c* sound, the children can raise their arms in the air above their heads. Creating various sounds and tones while practicing patterning is a fine way to connect math and music. Children will acquire much-needed early arithmetic skills by incorporating simple math patterns into music and movement.

Closing the Bloomin' Flowers Theme

Throughout your work with summer's Bloomin' Flowers activities, ask children questions to increase their comprehension. In your group times, be sure to discuss the purpose of flowers, what pollination is, and its importance. Here are some additional questions you can use during activities and to bring this theme to a close:

Why are flowers important?
Why do they have certain smells?
What else do we know about flowers?

Learning from Nature, Beyond Academics

When I feel stressed and need a temporary escape, I like to be near water. Often I will take a short walk to my pond. There is something very calming about hearing water trickle over rocks and seeing the white sparkle of sunshine reflecting on water. I take it all in and breathe the fresh air. From this space, I let go of stress and focus on the moment, releasing unnecessary worry. A tranquil peace enters my spirit and mind, making life clear—clear like water. After that, I am ready to return (or not return) to whatever I was fretful about. I am able to manage my concerns from an emotionally healthy place.

Mysticism celebrates nature and the wonderful healing effects it provides. We know instinctively that being with nature is good for us, and researchers continue to try to determine exactly why. Even without knowing exactly *why*, we know it is good to include nature in our lives.

We have discussed how important nature is for children. We have taken the children outdoors, we have integrated nature into the classroom, and we have tried our best to get families on board. It is equally important to connect with nature ourselves. Who each of us is as a person affects the world around us—the children we work with, our friends, and our family. With all of nature's power and secrets, think about these questions for yourself:

How can nature help me when stress appears in my life?
What simple things can I do within nature to create more peace in my surrounding world?
Better yet, how can I proactively include nature in my everyday life?

In this chapter, you will find straightforward and down-to-earth ideas for integrating nature into your own and the children's lives. These ideas will take you outside the typical classroom activity and into the remarkable benefits of nature, where you can make clearer sense of your world.

Scheduling Quality Time in Nature

Nature is important, and we must not forget to spend time within it. Nature refreshes the mind and the body, and a refreshed mind thinks wisely. A rejuvenated body works better. What time can *you* make for *yourself* in nature? Create some "me" time, and make it happen!

Share with children the importance of actually scheduling time in nature. Remind them how nature can help us emotionally when we are upset, and physically when we need to be revitalized. Ask the children *when* they will spend time outdoors. Emphasize how important it is to shut off all electronic devices, that it is important to be immersed in nature. Have meaningful conversations with them about nature and within nature. When children experience its calming benefits together, they will inevitably be grateful for nature. When they discover how it renews itself and feel the miracle of a fresh season together, they will appreciate the experience even more. Together we end up teaching each other how to be in awe of nature's power: the storms, the rainbows, the oceans, right down to our wonder at a unique snowflake or the details of a delicate flower. Quality time equals preciousness; quality time is life.

Healing Conflicts with Nature's Help

It is important to teach children that one aspect of life is having ups and downs. Conflicts happen. When children are quite emotional or on the edge of having temper tantrums, take them outdoors to resolve their conflicts with one another. This works best when you can give your attention to the children involved and a colleague can supervise the others.

When working to resolve conflict between children, bring their attention to their breathing. Model how to sit in a comfortable position facing each other. Point out the moment by asking them to close their eyes and be aware with their other senses—what it smells like outdoors, how the air and ground feel, and what sounds are nearby. Ask them to feel the ground beneath them and the air on their skin, and to listen to the sounds around them. All this will help them focus on the world around them instead of the frenzy within.

Tell them to take a few deep breaths. Next, tell them to open their eyes and notice the person sitting across from them. Share your hope that they can work things out with another. Explain that now that they are calm, you want them to use their words to discuss what is bothering them. Say that once their conflict is resolved, they can go back to doing what they were doing (children always want to go back to doing what they were doing, so this will motivate them to find a solution). Have them talk independently. Doing so gives them conflict resolution skills. In the meantime, they've experienced a brief meditative exercise and time in nature, both of which are priceless.

As adults, we, too, can practice taking a few moments outdoors for ourselves. When your fired up about a situation, go outside. Inhale the peace of nature into your heart. Calm your emotions, and return to the external conflict with a piece of nature's serenity in your spirit. If emotionally possible, ask the other person in conflict to peacefully walk outside with you. Be within the harmony of nature, the calmness it provides. While in that healthy space, you can try your best to discuss the conflict with an even-tempered attitude, with the relaxed stance of your wisdom. Remember, it is always best within any situation, especially those that are overly stressful, to be even-tempered and present within the moment. The more you practice being composed and tolerant, the better it is for everyone involved.

Resolving Internal Conflict

Resolving internal conflict is a mature skill. Many adults I know work very hard at this skill. Others continue carrying internal conflict throughout life. Regardless of your ability or expertise, it is important to practice this skill. Doing so in nature moves the process of conflict resolution along in a healthy, natural manner. All individuals of all ages can be taught the basics of resolving internal conflict. The foundation lies within the presence of nature. The present moment does not hold grudges, does not reflect on the past, and does not predict the future. Rather, the focus is on the now and how awesome aliveness feels in the now. Notice this and how we can learn from it and release internal conflict from this peaceful space.

We can teach the children we work with to be present by bringing their attention to breathing. Taking a breath in nature adds gratefulness to the heart. In my parenting, I used to have my children run to the tree and back when they were upset or angry. I learned that time in nature, whether you are the parent or the child, can calm all types of behavior and thinking, whether it is irrational, distracted, angry, agitated, or simply wound up. When you add quiet time, breathing time, and attention to the moment in nature, you have resolution and reflection at its optimum.

As an adult, I have realized that many of my best ideas have come to me while personally reflecting in nature. Take time to teach children how to simply spend time and enjoy life in nature. This in itself is a wonderful way for children to settle their internal conflicts.

Here is an exercise for resolving internal conflict in nature. You can use it for yourself and you can teach it to others; it is emotionally beneficial for everyone.

Imagine your breath in nature, and notice what comes to your mind. While in nature's space, notice your thoughts and watch those thoughts dissipate into the air. Continue breathing and practice letting go of any feelings, judgments, or thoughts. Always turn your attention back to your breath, to every inhale and to every exhale. Continue with the practice of letting go of all thoughts, bringing the focus back to this very moment in nature, and the breath.

This practice sounds simple, but it takes great discipline. It is worthwhile because it benefits the spirit. We can learn how to be more even tempered and patient in every circumstance. We can practice being more even-tempered and more patient with every child. When we learn how to be present, we can then teach children how to do so as well.

Being in the moment and teaching about it is another one of nature's greatest gifts. It is about presence. We have heard it said time and again: we are human beings, not human doings. This is a fine adage to offer to children. And it is a fine approach to follow ourselves.

Here is another simple meditative exercise I do on a regular basis. You can do it anytime you're outside, while walking on a path or sitting on a porch swing. Try it for yourself, and notice the difference in your outlook and feelings. As positive thoughts enter your mind, inhale them and picture them flowing into your heart and through your entire being. As negative thoughts enter your mind, exhale and let go of them. Notice yourself sending them back out to the universe, dispersing them, and visualizing them dissolving into the air. Inhaling only positive thoughts and exhaling all negativity is adding a bit of meditative reflection in nature.

If you do not make ample time for reflecting in nature, you can still try it while simply walking into your school building. It works well on frosty mornings as well as summer afternoons. Calmness benefits everyone.

Harmony in the Classroom

I also have found that bringing nature into my classroom helps my students and me. I have painted rocks on my desk for paper-weights (the ones we created in the spring Finding Stones theme) and worry stones to handle and fiddle with before heading to a long meeting or a challenging parent-teacher conference. I also include worry stones for the children to use in our thinking area to touch and practice as they let go of anxieties. The thinking area is a small space in the classroom where children can sit and reflect when they need to. And throughout the year during classroom center time, I bring in snow, rainwater, leaves, flowers, and other nature items for the children to explore and enjoy.

In what ways could you add more nature, a slice of serenity, to your teaching life? Are there nature ideas you can easily incorporate into your classroom design? What nature-filled inspirations can you create to help you personally in your occupation? Try adding more nature to your professional surroundings. You will be pleased with the tranquillity it offers you.

Harmony at Home

Nature continues to be a vital and healthy component in my personal life. Nature has helped me with my parenting. When my children were little and they became cranky or tired, I used nature as a calming presence. A walk outside or some sitting time in the grass gave us the relaxed and peaceful feeling we needed.

The inside of my house includes plants in virtually every room. I have balancing stones in my bedroom, along with a small rock water fountain that sits on a large slate fieldstone. In other rooms throughout my home, I have bowls of interesting rocks and shells that I or my family have found on our travels. I try to bring the serenity of nature into my home. I also spend time landscaping outside my house. I plant flowers, decorate with rocks, make stone paths, and create vegetable gardens, all of which bring more harmony to my life.

Spending time outdoors and including nature in personal spaces are excellent strategies for not burning out in one of the most challenging jobs there is—teaching! When I leave for work in the morning from my home, where I cherish nature's tranquillity, I enter my classroom coming from a healthy space. I am ready for the bursting energy and the heavy workload of children.

To create a peaceful haven for yourself, consider what nature ideas you can incorporate into your own home. What nature space can you create and tune into in the morning before you enter the world of teaching? Simple gestures will add balance and harmony to all areas of your life, and incorporating nature's wisdom into our whole selves is what will benefit us as teachers most. What other ways can we support children to include more nature in their daily lives? How can we help children make nature a positive lifelong habit and tool?

Celebrate Each Season

I live in upstate New York, where the winters are long, and I like to celebrate spring by getting outdoors and honoring my home. I begin by cleaning up the old winter debris around the lawn and finish the day with a pleasant walk outdoors, which reminds me about the beauty and miracle of the season ahead. As summer follows, one of my favorite ways to bring in the warmest season is to have a big barbecue with all the fixings. I also make sure the hammock gets hung up. And because the hammock comes down when autumn first appears, I have to do something really special in fall, or I would dwell on missing my relaxing hammock time. Making a great autumn meal that includes my favorite butternut squash soup and a dessert of homemade apple crisp usually does the trick. When winter arrives, I sometimes hold candlelight gatherings for friends and family in my home for the winter solstice celebration.

As the official arrival of each season approaches, find your own personal way to bring in the season. Share it with others and discuss it with the children as well. Talk about all the ways to launch the season. I always like to use this phrasing: "How we bring in the season sets the tone for our season ahead." Phrasing it that way allows children to grasp that they have power over their attitude and actions. Setting the tone for the season, for the year, or for whatever is in front of you has a prevailing effect on your life.

Nature is more than a delight; it is mysterious abundance. Nature provides you with a collection of tools you can use your whole life. It calms, it heals, it is delicate and strong at the same time, and it prevails despite changing circumstances. Nature teaches, and its life lessons are better than any artificial creation.

Raise your glasses with me, celebrating nature's sustenance in gratitude. Cheer with me in thankfulness and appreciation as we head out to one of the most important jobs in the world, educating children. Here's to the seasons ahead, all of the surprises they will offer, all of the effects and magic they have for our children and for us. Here's to life and to celebrating nature!

Angela Schmidt Fishbaugh, author of *Seeking Balance in an Unbalanced World: A Teacher's Journey,* is on a mission to help today's world. Her passion is educating others on healthy balance and joyful living. She provides workshops for communities, teacher centers, parents, and caretakers on the topic of balance, and is a national presenter for The National Association for Family Child Care (NAFCC). Her motivational wellness strategies encourage others to live a healthy, balanced, and sound life. Angela aspires to help those who work with our greatest resource, the children. Visit Angela's website: www.balanceteacher.com.